Preparing
for
◆-College-◆

Preparing for College is the place to begin the college search. It offers the most comprehensive approach available to selecting the academic and social experience that best suits each individual. The authors, who each have more than 40 years of experience dealing with college fits and misfits, reveal the common misperceptions that can lead to bad choices.

— *Tom Curley*
President and CEO, The Associated Press

Picking a college may be the most under-informed decision most people make. . . . In *Preparing for College* Rooney and Reardon help students and their parents shift this choice from rash to rational.

— *Dennis O'Brien*
President Emeritus, University of Rochester

Of particular value is the authors' encouragement that college be viewed as an "investment rather than a cost." Through this lens, they offer practical advice on how to acquire the information necessary to determine the college that is right for each person and to manage the academic and social challenges of college.

— *Robert J. Thompson, Jr., Ph.D.*
Dean of Trinity College of Arts and Sciences, Duke University

I wish *Preparing for College* had been available to me when I began this journey myself! How wonderful it is that no one else has to just "survive" the college experience. Instead, you can thrive, based on this book.

— *Margaret Watson, Ph.D.*
Associate Dean, Graduate and Professional Studies, University of Houston

Preparing for College is a clear, concise guideline of what to think about in the context of the most precious transition that parents and their children will make: becoming the adults that you had always known they could be.

— *Tom O'Malia*
Director of the Lloyd Greif Center for Entrepreneurial Studies,
University of Southern California

Preparing
for
◆ College ◆

*Practical Advice for
Students and Their Families*

JOHN J. ROONEY, PH.D.
*Emeritus Professor Of Psychology
La Salle University*

JOHN F. REARDON, ED.D.
*Emeritus Professor Of Accounting
La Salle University*

FOREWORD BY
KATHERINE HALEY WILL
*President, Gettysburg College
Chair, Annapolis Group*

Checkmark Books®
An imprint of Infobase Publishing

We dedicate this book to our wives, Marion and Cathy,
for their love and inspiration throughout the years.

❦

Preparing for College: Practical Advice for Students and Their Families

Copyright © 2009 by John J. Rooney and John F. Reardon

Checkmark Books
An imprint of Facts On File, Inc.
132 West 31st Street
New York NY 10001

Library of Congress Cataloging-in-Publication Data

Rooney, John J.
  Preparing for college : practical advice for students and their families / John J. Rooney,
John F. Reardon ; foreword by Katherine Haley Will.
     p. cm.
  Includes bibliographical references and index.
  ISBN-13: 978-0-8160-7377-1 (hardcover : alk. paper)
  ISBN-10: 0-8160-7377-5 (hardcover : alk. paper)
  ISBN-13: 978-0-8160-7378-8 (pbk. : alk. paper)
  ISBN-10: 0-8160-7378-3 (pbk. : alk. paper) 1. College student orientation—United
States. 2. Education—Parent participation—United States. I. Reardon, John F. II. Title.
  LB2343.32.R66 2008
  378.1'98—dc22   2008009025

Checkmark Books are available at special discounts when purchased in bulk quantities
for businesses, associations, institutions, or sales promotions. Please call our Special
Sales Department in New York at (212) 967-8800 or (800) 322-8755.

You can find Facts On File on the World Wide Web at http://www.factsonfile.com

Text design by Mary Susan Ryan-Flynn
Cover design by Takeshi Takahashi

Printed in the United States of America

MP MSRF 10 9 8 7 6 5 4 3 2

This book is printed on acid-free paper.

CONTENTS

Foreword: Choosing a College: It's All About Fit ix

Preface. xi

1 Getting Ready for College. .1

Challenges for Today's Students 2

Big Decisions. 3

Advice for Parents 3

Advice for Students 4

2 Common Mistakes and How to Avoid Them 11

Overemphasis on Cost. 12

Overemphasis on Prestige .12

Overemphasis on the "Glitz" 14

Perfectionism 14

Starting Late 15

Failure to Plan a Visit 16

Underemphasizing Quality of Teaching and Learning . 16

Underestimating Your Potential. 16

Parental Domination 17

Excessive Peer Influence 18

Common Misconceptions About College 18

3 Handling the Cost of College 23

The Cost: Public Versus Private 23

Four or Five Years to Graduate? 24

Earnings in the Fifth Year. 25

Strategies to Reduce Costs. 27

Financial Aid. 29

Sources of Aid: Grants and Scholarships 30
ROTC Scholarships and Veterans Benefits 35
Tax Credits. 35
Loans. 36
Work 39
Savings 39
Steps in Applying for Aid 43
Comparing Financial Aid Packages 44

4 Picking a Major and Planning a Career. 51
Difficulties in Selecting a Career 52
Sources of Assistance. 53
A Tentative Major. 53
Career Choice and Major 54
Changing Majors. 55
The Value of a Liberal Arts Education. 56
Dos and Don'ts for Family 57
Career Counselors 59
High School Counselors 59
Private Professional Counselors 60
College Counselors 61
Predicting the Future. .61

5 The Right College, Not the Best College 63
The Steak or the Sizzle. 63
Universities Versus Colleges. 64
College Demands and Expectations 65
Competitive or Cooperative Atmosphere 65
Undergraduate Teaching Quality. 66
The College Curriculum 67
Educational and Social Considerations 67
Community Colleges and Distance Learning 73
Crime on Campus 74
Narrowing Your Choice 75
The College Visit 76
When the Right College Turns Out to Be Wrong 79

6 How to Get Accepted and More **81**

    The Application Process 82

    The Application 83

    Personal Statement 84

    Letters of Recommendation 85

    The Selection Interview 87

    Taking Admissions Tests 88

    Mathematics 91

    Writing 93

    Critical Reading 95

    Applied Knowledge 95

7 Academic Success and Its Value **99**

    Preparing for Academic Success 99

    Making the Transition to College 100

    Responsibilities in College 100

    The Value and Limitation of Grades 103

    Self-Discipline and Learning 104

    Basic Principles of Success in College 105

    Study Skills and the Learning Process 108

    Becoming an Active Learner 110

    Working with Your Professors 111

    Other Learning Resources 113

    Writing Papers 115

    Steps in Writing a Paper 115

    Emotional Maturity and Academic Performance 117

8 Personal and Emotional Maturity: the Social Side
**   of College** **121**

    Personal Development 121

    Role Models and Mentors 125

    Friends 125

    Roommates 126

    Dorm Life 127

    Parties 128

    Extracurricular Activities 130

Fraternities and Sororities 130
Athletics 131
Work Experience 132
Service Learning 132
Moral Development 133
Acquiring Life Skills. 134
Managing Money 134
Dealing with Over-Involved Parents. 135
Finding Your Personal Highway 136

9 A Safe and Healthy College Experience **139**
Accidents 139
Infectious Disease 140
Fire Safety 141
College Crime 141
Health Habits. 142
Sexuality. 144
Relationships. 146
Mental Health 147
Body Image. 149
Drug and Alcohol Use at College 151
Drug Dangers 160

10 The Role of Inspiration and Commitment **163**
The Experience of Others .164
Historical Perspective 164
Sources of Inspiration 165
The Mayonnaise Jar and the Golf Balls 167
Never Give Up 168
If I Only Knew In College .169

Appendix: Online Sources for College Planning **171**

Bibliography **179**

Index **189**

About the Authors **195**

FOREWORD
Choosing a College: It's All About Fit

Preparing for College: Practical Advice for Students and Their Families is a good place to begin the important process of choosing a college. After several decades in a variety of higher education institutions, first as a student, then as a professor, an administrator, and ultimately as a college president, I am convinced that there is no one "right" college for every individual, there are many. We are so fortunate to have thousands of excellent colleges and universities from which to choose. Your job—in consultation with your family—is to winnow down the list of institutions to the ones that make the most sense for you.

There are lots of things to consider, and this book along with other college guides, Web sites, and your high school counselor, will help you sort through the options. Take your time and do your homework, because there is a lot of information to sort through. One note of caution: Although the annual college ratings list is fun to peruse, it is based on what many consider to be an inherently flawed methodology and should not be used as the basis for a decision as important as where to go to college.

As you narrow your list, one thing I would strongly recommend is a campus visit. Very little can replace experiencing a college "in the flesh." All of the Web sites and blogs, ratings lists, and suggestions of friends are no substitute for talking to current students, walking around campus, and sitting in on a class. Take the guided tour but also walk around by yourself, engage people in conversation, walk around the library, sit in student gathering spots. Can you imagine yourself in this place?

Remember, there are many environments in which each student can thrive. When all the basics have been reviewed, look inside your heart and listen to your gut. Where a college ranks, whether friends think it's "cool," how prestigious it is—none of these considerations addresses who you are and who you have the potential to become. College is not a prize to be won; it's an experience to be lived and from which to learn. In the final analysis, which campus feels "right"—where you can see yourself being happy—is more important.

—Katherine Haley Will
President, Gettysburg College
Chair, Annapolis Group

PREFACE

Every year several million high school juniors and seniors are faced with the task of deciding whether to go on to college, which college to attend, what to major in, how to get accepted, and how to pay for a college education. Some of them decide, often without good reasons, to skip college. Some of them do not get accepted by their first-choice college. Many do not claim the financial aid for which they are eligible because they are unaware that they qualify for it. Others choose a school and course of study only to later change colleges or majors or drop out altogether.

This book is designed to help high school students get accepted into the colleges that are right for them, obtain the financial aid for which they are eligible, and select an appropriate major. It also aims to help first-year college students get the most out of their college experience.

Parents and students are naturally concerned with the cost of college. In fact, they are often overwhelmed with sticker shock when they see the list price of college tuition, room and board, and other expenses. The process of obtaining financial aid, including scholarships, grants, assistantships, and low-interest loans is a major project. Parents need help. We have therefore spelled out procedures for determining the true cost of attending college, while also emphasizing that college is an investment in the future and that selecting the right college, not the best college (nor the least or most expensive) is an important step in that investment.

Numerous articles in magazines and newspapers discuss the need for a systematic and thorough approach to the college search process. In searching the Internet, we found a significant number of hits relating to the essence of our book. In recent years, *Newsweek*, *U.S. News & World Report*, and *Time* have covered this topic, and daily newspapers also regularly feature articles on planning for college. Most of them focus on one specific aspect of the search process; we believe we have covered everything a student and his or her family needs. Simply put, this book is one-stop shopping.

In addition to being a source of useful factual information, the authors provide the voice of experience. Each of the authors has 40 or more years of university teaching experience, and we have learned a great deal from working with our students. We have shared in their hopes and concerns, their struggles and uncertainties, their failures and successes. Our goal is to convey this experience to the next generation of college students. We encourage students to learn to make wise choices, while realizing that they will probably make some poor choices along the way, and that they can learn much from such mistakes. We also believe that the college search process itself can be a valuable source of personal growth.

Arguably, the greatest period of maturation, intellectual development, personal focus, stabilized perspective, and ultimately, fulfillment begins in the college years. This book is a primer in helping students and parents deal with this process, including the anxieties involved in leaving home and coping with the rigors of the collegiate environment.

We hope that reading this book will help you make your college years more enjoyable and more successful.

Chapter 1

Getting Ready for College

Something of value that is sought by many, often given freely, but seldom taken: advice.

—*Source Unknown*

Youth can learn much from the mistakes of their elders, but seem determined to make their own.

—*Source Unknown*

As a student who is getting ready for college, you face both opportunities and challenges. You are confronting rocketing scientific and technological advances, a shifting global economy, and political and international strife. Like students from previous generations, you are concerned with what lies ahead. You may look forward to a successful career, a happy family, and a fulfilling life, yet you are anxious about the future.

Your parents and other family members are also interested and concerned about your plans. They recognize that this is a pivotal point in your life; they want to be helpful, but are often uncertain about what is best for you. They also know that you are becoming more mature and ready to take a more active role in decisions about your future.

This book is intended to help you and your family get the most out of college and prepare for the future with both a realistic and an optimistic view.

Studies of what makes people successful and happy, as mentioned in Barry Schwartz's *The Paradox of Choice*, show that those who always want the best (maximizers) are more successful; however, those who settle for a good outcome, if not necessarily the best one (satisficers), are happier. We hope, as you prepare for college, that the suggestions in this book will help you find both success and happiness.

CHALLENGES FOR TODAY'S STUDENTS

Commentators differ in their assessments of the present generation of high school students. Some observers see them as overwhelmed with excessive homework and teacher and parental demands to do more to embellish their résumés in preparation for college. College teachers, on the other hand, in informal reports and on faculty list-servs, generally see them as not measuring up to the task of college courses. Anecdotally, common complaints are that "they don't know the basics" and "expect high marks without doing the work." A third view, focusing on how today's college student is saturated in information, is presented in an article by Michael L. Rogers and David A. Starrett of Southwest Missouri State University:

> He sits at his computer with headphones piping music from an iPod to his ears. Ten different MSN chat windows blink and chime on the computer screen. An online role-playing game is minimized on the Windows taskbar. A music video blares from a TV in a corner of the room. A calculus book lies nonchalantly open by the cell phone, which itself sits next to the PC. He is doing his homework. He is real. He is a Twenty-First Century Learner.
>
> The first of these learners are now graduating from college. Many more are making their way through the K-12 system and into college. They have expectations, needs, and wants shaped by a childhood spent in a tech-enabled environment. Such characteristics as multi-tasking, a preference for visual modes of communication, a need for instant gratification, and a strong desire for social connectedness partly define how they learn. The technology-enhanced world in which we live has impacted their development as individuals and as learners.

Whichever view of today's students fits you (or if you are some combination of all three) you still must make your way through the same processes previous generations have negotiated in taking the next step in your education.

BIG DECISIONS

High school students planning to attend college face a number of decisions: which college to attend, how to apply and get accepted, what major to select, how to pay for college, what activities to become involved in, and how to make college a meaningful, worthwhile, and enjoyable experience.

Like many rites of passage, the transition from high school to college presents a number of intellectual, social, emotional, and financial challenges. You must decide how to meet the challenges you face and use the opportunities that are available, how to set priorities among the variety of activities in which you are involved, and how to pay for your expenses without incurring excessive debt.

ADVICE FOR PARENTS

A wise man once said: "You want to give your kids two things. One is roots, and the other is wings." By sending your children off to college, you are setting them aloft on their journey of life. It hurts, but would you want it any other way?

Please remember that in August, as you drive away from the university, leaving your son or daughter behind for the first time, there will be lumps in your throat and tears on your cheeks. That is to be expected. But your sons and daughters will return home in a few short months for winter break. They will be different people than the ones you left behind on that August day. But here is the good news! As your children depart again in mid-January to return to school, there will be fewer or no tears on your cheeks and perhaps no lumps in your throat. You may even break out the wine and turn on the music! The proverbial umbilical cord will have been officially severed. Your sons or daughters will always be your children, but they no longer share the same nest with you. Their pursuit of becoming independent, self-sustaining young adults has officially begun.

ADVICE FOR STUDENTS

You will be a different person several years from now when you are finishing college and getting ready to begin your career. Your expectation may be that you will be a better person, and probably you will. Whether or not you are, however, depends largely on the kind of choices you make and the lifestyle you adopt during your college years.

The college selection process is a good place to start. It can be a valuable learning experience, teaching you how to plan ahead, organize your time, acquire pertinent information and assistance, meet deadlines, and accomplish a complex task. It can be a period of uncertainty, but if you approach it with openness and humor you should do well. When you have completed the process, you should feel that you have made important decisions that are good for you, and that you are now better prepared to make decisions about your life in the future.

Keep in mind that what is right for your friends and classmates may not be right for you. Students have a wide variety of backgrounds, abilities, and interests, as well as many options regarding where to attend college and what to study. The following are brief vignettes of a few high school students and their plans. Each of them is making some common mistakes in preparing for college. As you read through the cases, consider how you would advise them to improve their planning. We will discuss this more in the next chapter.

Throughout this book we use examples of students to illustrate a point. We have typically either modified the case to protect the identity of the person or used a composite based on several individuals.

Steve

Steve is planning to attend engineering school. He has always liked working with machines and tinkering with mechanical things. Generally, he has done well in high school, but, although he knows you need mathematics for engineering, he doesn't like math and hasn't done well in it. Some parts of science he enjoys, like the lab work, but he finds the theory pretty dull. He spends a lot of time working on his car. It is three years old but looks new and runs great. He also wants to learn more about airplanes, and maybe take flying lessons.

Annette

She has done fairly well in a Catholic high school with a good academic reputation. Her main interest, however, has been athletics. She plays on the softball and field hockey teams and plans to continue playing in college. Several of her friends are planning to attend a private Catholic college in a nearby state. She is impressed with their brochures and Web site. It looks like a really nice place. She is undecided on a major, but will figure that out somewhere along the way. She is looking forward to college, although she will miss her family. It should be fun.

Howard

Only a few of his friends are going to college. Most of them are anxious to get a full-time job and start making some money. Still, he believes if you want to get ahead in this society, you have to "do the college thing."

Basketball is his main interest. He didn't get any kind of athletic scholarship, even though he believes he is just as good as most guys who did get one. He intends to find more time to practice and make the team as a walk-on. He is thinking of majoring in sociology or business management.

Caitlin

She is attending a private prep school. Her parents and teachers have emphasized that she must obtain excellent grades and develop an impressive record of achievement if she wants to get into one of the top-tier colleges. She has studied abroad during summer sessions, taken advanced placement (AP) courses, gotten tutoring to prepare for the Scholastic Assessment Test (SAT), and done volunteer work in a children's hospital. She is interested in science, but uncertain of the area of specialization. Her senior year has been hectic for her and most of her friends. There are so many activities, and so much pressure, that she is anxious and tense much of the time. At times she feels like quitting the rat race. She wonders if maybe she and her boyfriend Mark should get married, forget about college, and go live on a farm.

Jonathan

High school has been easy for him, but Jonathan doesn't consider himself a "brain." He is just a regular guy who likes to play sports and go out with friends. Still, he always did well on standardized tests. He does like to read, particularly, biographies and science fiction, and enjoys playing chess and computer games. He plans to go to the local community college. His English teacher, who seems like a knowledgeable guy, thinks he should apply to some other colleges and try for a scholarship. That seems unrealistic to Jonathan. His friends say you need to be some kind of genius to get an academic scholarship.

Allison

Has a part-time job as a waitress. This has made it hard to excel in high school, but her grades have been above average. She is uncertain whether to go on to college full time or take some courses in the evening. Either way, she would live at home and commute to a local public college. Finances will be tight if she attends college full time, but she and her parents do not want to take out a loan. Rather, she would increase her hours at work and earn enough for tuition and other expenses. This won't leave much time for study or recreation, but she thinks she can get by. Allison has thought of becoming a teacher or a nurse, but is unsure.

Meredith

Meredith's father and mother are highly successful attorneys. They both attended a prestigious and highly competitive college, and she has always planned to go there, too. Although she has worked hard in school, her grades are not much above average. Her scores on the PSAT and SAT were also a bit low for her chosen college. Still, she expects to get admitted because her father and mother are influential alumni. Meredith is also planning to become a lawyer. It seems like a good life. Her aunt, who works as a paralegal in the law firm, isn't so sure she is making a wise choice. She thinks she should consider other options.

Ben

Ben is looking forward to college and is planning to have a lot of fun. The state university has strong football and basketball teams and a reputation for lots of parties. Ben is going to follow a major in television communication and maybe be a sports announcer. He is sure he would like this, but career plans can come later, after he is through college. Right now he just wants to get away from home to someplace where he can do what he feels like doing. Ben's parents argue a lot and may be getting a divorce. "Oh well," he thinks, "that's their problem." He broke up with his girlfriend recently. She was getting to be a pain because of the way she criticized him and said he was drinking too much.

Jerry

Ever since he can remember, Jerry has been expected to go to Notre Dame. His father, a policeman, is a big Notre Dame fan and so is Jerry. As far as Jerry is concerned, it's Notre Dame or nothing, or rather, no other college. His high school grades have been fairly good, but he knows he could have done better. He is determined to work harder now that he is a senior and get the kind of grades that will get him accepted and also get the financial help he will need. If he doesn't get accepted at Notre Dame, he will skip college and try to get on the police force.

If we take a quick look at each of the above students, we can see ways they can improve their approach to college planning.

Steve has selected engineering despite below average performance in math and a limited interest in science. He will likely have difficulty getting accepted in an engineering program, and, if he does get in, he will probably have trouble completing the program. Does this mean he should forget about engineering? Not necessarily. A more thorough check of his aptitudes and a better understanding of the requirements and work life of the various specialties within engineering would help him with his decision. In Chapter 4 we discuss the use of career counseling for such students.

Annette has made the mistake of picking a college without making a visit. We discuss the importance of the college visit, and how to get the most out of it in Chapter 5.

Howard seems to be focusing on athletics and minimizing the importance of academics. In chapters 7 and 8 we discuss the need for students to set priorities during college and to strike an appropriate balance among the various demands of college life.

Caitlin is an example of a student who is under the pressure of preparing for highly competitive colleges and majors. For some students this is desirable, but others would be better served aiming for a less-competitive college with a sound reputation. We discuss this dilemma in several places throughout the book, particularly in Chapter 5.

Jonathan is the kind of student who underestimates himself. By failing to apply for a competitive scholarship, he takes himself out of the running. This is a chance for him to test himself and find out more about his potential. In much of the book we encourage students to recognize their potential, particularly in Chapter 3, where we describe the various kinds of scholarships and other aid that is available and tell how to maximize your chances for obtaining such assistance.

Allison and her family seem to have ruled against taking out a low-interest loan without examining the advantages of doing so. In Chapter 3 we discuss college as an investment, rather than an expense, and indicate various ways of paying for it.

Meredith is planning on a highly competitive college and major, despite low achievement to date. Career counseling would be useful to see if law is a realistic choice and to help her examine other options if it is not. In Chapter 4, we discuss the value of professional career counseling, and how to find the counselor that is right for you.

Ben is headed toward a college experience that may not only be a waste of time, but a time in which he is liable to drift rapidly into a self-destructive lifestyle. Chapters 8 and 9 address these and related issues.

Jerry is making a couple of serious mistakes in his planning. First of all, he is limiting his choice to one college and basing that choice on the general reputation of the college rather than knowing whether it is a good fit for him. Secondly, even if he has a first choice that is right for him, he should have been able to find other colleges that would also give him an educational experience consistent with his plans in case he is not accepted by or cannot afford his first choice. A final mistake is in waiting until his senior year to put his time and energy into doing well in high school. That's generally too late. These issues are considered more fully in chapters 4, 5, and 6.

No doubt you can think of other high school students and notice some of the things they are doing (or not doing) in planning for college, including some things that are helpful and some that make it less likely that they will have a successful experience. Give some thought to your college preparations and those of your friends to see if any of you are making mistakes like those described above.

LOOKING AHEAD

In the next chapter we take a look at some common mistakes students and their families make in preparing for college and discuss how you can avoid them. In subsequent chapters, we give you suggestions on how to pay for college, how to select a major, how to find the best college for you, and how to get accepted there. We then look at how to get the most out of your college experience in terms of academic achievement, personal and social development, and your own health and safety. Finally, we tell you a few brief tales that we hope will provide some motivation and inspiration to take with you on your journey.

Chapter 2

Common Mistakes and How to Avoid Them

A man should never be ashamed to own he has been in the wrong, which is but saying, in other words, that he is wiser today than he was yesterday.

—*Jonathan Swift,* Thoughts on Various Subjects

A few years ago a graduate of Columbia University sued that institution. His complaint? He had paid to become an educated person, and the university had not, in fact, educated him.

The judge ruled against him on the grounds that Columbia had provided him with the *opportunity to obtain an education*, but he had not taken advantage of it. Not taking advantage of the opportunities available at college is probably the most common error that students make. Too many students are like the scarecrow in *The Wizard of Oz*: too convinced that it is the diploma in their hands, and not what they have in their heads, that counts.

College provides students with the opportunity for substantial intellectual and personal growth. Some students take advantage of this time in their lives and become mature, competent, and responsible individuals; others simply drift along, achieving little improvement or indeed even developing a lifestyle that makes it more difficult for them to be successful or satisfied with their lives.

Seizing opportunities in high school is equally important. An excellent record there is your ticket to "the big dance," so don't put off serious learning until college—or you may find yourself stopped at the door.

In planning for college, students and their families make a number of other common mistakes. It is helpful to be aware of these.

OVEREMPHASIS ON COST

College is expensive, but it is also one of the most valuable investments people can make. Some students and their families decide that they cannot afford to go to college, without really looking into the possibilities. Some look for the least expensive college, often without accurately evaluating the cost and benefits. Some even go mainly by the listed price or "sticker price" before considering either financial aid—which reduces the cost considerably—or whether it may take five years to graduate from a program, which increases the cost substantially.

Other decisions affecting cost include whether to commute from home or live on campus; whether to attend a public, private, or community college; and whether to be a part-time or a full-time student.

In the next chapter we discuss the cost of college and offer some ideas on how to utilize scholarships, assistantships, low-interest loans, and part-time work to pay for it.

OVEREMPHASIS ON PRESTIGE

If we ask, "What are the best colleges in the United States?" we can get general agreement on a number of highly selective institutions that have established a reputation for excellence over the years.

If a student asks, "Which are the best colleges for me?" the answer is much more elusive and seldom the same as the answer to the first question. A common mistake is to look for the *best college* rather than the *right college* or the *best match*. Highly selective, prestigious colleges are great places for some students; for others they spell disaster.

Some college students we know reported a striking example of how prestige can distort the college selection process. They were tutoring high school students from an inner-city school from which few graduates went on to college. Almost invariably, the students were interested in only one college: Harvard. Many of them said if they couldn't get into Harvard, it wasn't worth going to any other college.

Finding a college that is a great match for you takes a good bit of digging, but knowing that you are looking for the right college rather than the best college is a giant step in the right direction.

You must resist pressures to go to the most prestigious college that you can get into. Parents can also be drawn into this kind of one-upmanship, seeing their child's achievement as a reflection of their own success. High school teachers and administrators often overemphasize the number of graduates from their school who have been accepted into prestigious colleges, rather than on how they have helped all of their graduates make wise choices.

Highly Competitive Colleges

Students are often under considerable stress in college. They face the demands of difficult courses, living away from home and family, and the challenges of normal development, peer pressure, social relationships, and planning for an uncertain future.

For many students the pressures of succeeding academically and being accepted socially in a highly competitive atmosphere adds too much stress for them to benefit from the experience. Excessive stress is one of the main reasons for low student performance, emotional distress, and dropping out of college. A certain amount of stress is normal in any situation, and most young people learn to respond to it through extra effort and more efficient work habits. When stress is excessive, however, it produces tension and frustration that interfere with effective learning.

On the other hand, some students do have the talent and personal resources to thrive under pressure, including some who do not recognize their potential. One example is Jonathan, described in Chapter 1, who minimized his achievements and was reluctant to apply for a highly competitive scholarship. "Sure I can get good grades," he said "but I'm no brain. I'm just a regular, ordinary guy." He did decide to apply just to see what would happen and was accepted. In college, he enjoyed competing with and usually doing better than "the brains."

Moreover, students feel social pressure to be accepted by the group. This is particularly stressful at schools where most of a student's peers may be from prestigious prep schools, belong to exclusive sororities or fraternities, or drive Porsches and Mercedes Benzes.

A student who has a job waiting on tables and drives a used car may feel a sense of isolation or rejection in such a setting.

Friendly Colleges

At the other extreme is the student who gravitates to a college that many of his or her friends are attending. She eats lunch and socializes with the same group as in high school and is basically in grade 13 in the educational system. This may feel comfortable, but it provides little opportunity for the growth that occurs from interacting with students from varied backgrounds and with different intellectual and social perspectives. Don't just drift into a college to be with friends. Look for one that is challenging and at the same time provides the kind of support that helps you meet the challenges.

OVEREMPHASIS ON THE "GLITZ"

It has been said that some colleges are "built on a bluff and run the same way." In choosing a college, too many families are overly impressed with superficial amenities. Others reflect on how they made this mistake in the university they chose.

Huge football stadiums and elaborate student union buildings give little indication of important characteristics of the university. In fact, they are often accompanied by huge classrooms where students are mere spectators, just as they are at the athletic events.

Other colleges offer more opportunity for students to be active participants in classes, athletics, and other extracurricular activities.

PERFECTIONISM

Some students develop the feeling that no matter what they do, it is not enough. They see the college admissions process as a contest in which others are doing more and are ahead of them in the competition. They have an exaggerated sense of missing out on something and a fear of being left out. They are under constant pressure to not make mistakes and to do more and more. Parents sometimes unwittingly foster this attitude rather than encouraging a more realistic and balanced approach.

Deciding on a college and a major should be a process guided by a clear understanding of your goals, talents, and interests, and facilitated by learning about the opportunities available to you. You should strive not for perfection, but for openness, initiative, and curiosity. Listen to your heart!

STARTING LATE

Procrastination is a common problem. "Never put off until tomorrow what you can put off until next week" seems to be the motto of many young people.

Deciding on a college and picking a major seem so daunting and produce so much anxiety that students may put off doing these

LOCATION, LOCATION, LOCATION

Being able to get home from college regularly has its advantages. In fact, The New York Times reported that, historically, evidence suggests that students are less likely to drop out of college if they are within 250 miles from home. If you live in Philadelphia and choose to go away to college, applying the 250-mile rule might surprise you. If you drive north you are near Boston; west you are close to eastern Ohio; south you are in Virginia. (But watch out—250 miles east gets you wet!) A list of the schools within this region would be very impressive in terms of the quality, variety, and eclectic mix of institutions available. The lesson here is to consider schools that allow easy weekend visits home.

Location can be overemphasized, however. Today, students can get home from most parts of the country in one day. There is some expense and inconvenience involved with long-distance travel, but it may be worth it to attend the right college.

things. The solution is to break the process into smaller steps and deal with them one at a time. Set up a schedule so you take care of each step in a timely fashion. If you are uncertain, it usually helps to make a tentative decision and proceed. If you later change your mind, you can make the needed adjustments.

A late start in planning for college leads to additional tension, difficulty in making wise decisions, and missed opportunities. It is never too early to start the process. Serious planning should begin at least by the junior year in high school. That is the appropriate time for narrowing the search process, including making visits to colleges that you are considering.

FAILURE TO PLAN A VISIT

Although you can get considerable information about colleges from brochures, Web sites, and other sources, visiting a college before making a decision is a must. Plan carefully for your visit so you get the information you need to make a wise choice. Recommendations for college visits are discussed more fully in Chapter 5, "The Right College, Not the Best College."

UNDEREMPHASIZING QUALITY OF TEACHING AND LEARNING

In college visits, arrange to sit in on classes, stay in a residence hall, and talk with students about the nature of the teaching. Check on the size of the classes and the teaching ability of the faculty or teaching assistants who are actually doing the teaching. In particular, meet with students and faculty in your prospective major and see whether their experience is a good match with your expectations.

UNDERESTIMATING YOUR POTENTIAL

Having taught undergraduates for more than 80 years combined, the authors believe that a strong work ethic is a more important factor in achieving academic success than a high ACT or SAT score. The teenager who grows up with news magazines on the kitchen table, who vacations in Europe, and who enrolls in costly ACT or SAT prep courses will usually do better on the test than others. This may not be fair, but it is also not that important. High ACT or SAT scores do not necessarily translate into excellence in the classroom, in part because there are cognitive abilities that are not measured by these tests, and in part because achievement in college is influenced as much by non-intellectual traits. Although a brilliant intellect may carry you far, good work habits will usually be rewarded more. The student who systematically studies with an unrelenting commitment to the mission of learning almost always outperforms the classmate with the high board scores and devil-may-care attitude. As psychologists Angela Duckworth and Martin Seligman say in summarizing the results of their research on achievement in adolescents: "True grit trumps I.Q. every time."

It is important to remember that substantial intellectual growth will take place during the four-year college experience. The ACT or SAT score is merely a means of ranking applicants, in very specific skills, as they embark on their journey forward. These scores do not indicate future difficulties in the college classroom unless a student allows them to damage his or her self-image, which may lead to a self-fulfilling prophecy of poor performance.

PARENTAL DOMINATION

Parents and other family members are usually involved in a helpful way in the college selection process. Students can use assistance in making the choice involved and in learning how to go about making such decisions. There are, however, cases in which parents dominate the process, and students are mainly passive participants. This usually leads to poor decisions and little student development. The student who is involved in the decision and makes a commitment to it is much more likely to become highly motivated to do the work required to succeed. A student who believes it is the parents' decision can readily believe that the outcome is also their responsibility. Remember that students at this stage in their lives are on the road to independence, even though they still need some support and direction in getting there.

Both students and parents typically find themselves under some stress during the college application process. Parents can be most helpful by handling this stress in a healthy way and setting a good example; they should avoid projecting their own anxiety onto the student. Instead, student and parents should work together. Taking time to listen to one another and to engage in some family activity that all enjoy can mean a great deal. Usually, the teenager needs some balance between academic work and social and leisure activity. It helps if parents can be encouraging and support the positive steps the student takes, rather than being critical of mistakes. It also helps if the student recognizes that parents are concerned and trying to be helpful, even when it comes across as criticism.

EXCESSIVE PEER INFLUENCE

At this stage in life, most high school students are influenced considerably by their peers. When it comes to the choice of college and major, listening to one's peers is often a case of the blind leading the blind. Some of your classmates will pass along bits of information, misinformation, and biases. Working with friends to exchange factual information can be helpful, but don't let yourself become concerned if your decisions about your college or your major will impress your friends. It's your future, so it should be *your* decision.

COMMON MISCONCEPTIONS ABOUT COLLEGE

I can't afford to attend college.

Actually you can't afford not to go to college. With few exceptions, a bachelor's degree is the ticket to admission to the world of work. You can't climb the mountain if you don't take that first step. Think of college as an investment in the rest of your professional life, not as a present-day expenditure.

High school is a time to have fun. I'll wait until I get to college to buckle down and study.

First of all, this attitude will limit your choice of colleges and programs because you will not have done well in high school. Secondly, the kind of habits you develop in setting priorities and scheduling times for study and recreation during high school tend to carry over into college.

I have to be an outstanding student or have very limited income to get financial aid.

Not true. Many private colleges use grants, loans, and work-study positions as vehicles to recruit their freshman classes. Schools compete to obtain students, and the more financial aid they can offer, the more students they can attract. All students, whatever their academic record or financial status, should investigate the opportunities for financial aid.

Getting into college is very difficult.

From the perspective of the anxiety-driven applicant, this may seem to be the case. In reality, just about every high school graduate can get into college. Getting into the right college for you and getting the most out of the college experience is clearly the hard and most important part.

It is better to take an easy program in high school and get better grades.

This is a big mistake. College admissions directors are much more likely to make decisions based on the rigor of high school courses taken than the grades. Any advanced placement (AP) or honors courses carry far more weight than good grades in easy courses.

The more activities I participate in the better.

The quality of the activities and your contribution to them is more important than the sheer quantity. Serving as editor of the school newspaper or yearbook is far more indicative of high potential than being a member of a variety of social clubs.

Senior year in high school doesn't matter much.

How you do in your senior year is a good indication of how you will do in college. To use a baseball analogy, would you judge a player using last year's statistics or those from two years ago? Although many decisions regarding admissions and financial aid are made before your final senior grades are available, these are subject to modification. In some cases, offers are withdrawn as a result of poor senior year grades, in other instances high achievement in the senior year leads to additional awards.

The PSAT, taken in the junior year, is just practice for the SAT.

This was the original idea, but it is now used in awarding Merit Scholarships and other kinds of aid.

I don't have to worry about my grades or courses until my junior year in high school.

The kind of classes you take in your freshman year and how well you do in them lays the foundation for your later work. Although students can recover from a poor start, preparation for college proceeds more smoothly if you make appropriate course selections and obtain good grades right from the beginning.

Summer is a good time to make college visits.

It is much better to visit colleges during the academic year when you can sit in on classes, stay in the residence facilities, and meet with students and faculty. It gives you a more accurate sense of the college experience.

I can't apply for financial aid until I know where I am going to college.

Actually, the inverse is more accurate. You can't decide where you are going to college until you know the amount of financial aid offered by each of the schools. The difference in the financial aid package among schools is often substantial.

SUMMARY

In this chapter we have highlighted some common mistakes made in preparing for college. Our intent is not to raise your anxiety about the process; rather, we want you to approach college planning with more confidence and satisfaction, and to avoid common missteps.

We are assuming you will go to college, and we believe that you should be looking forward to it with anticipation and enthusiasm.

The decisions you face are important, but not critical. Do you attend University A or B? It's possible that either school would be a positive and fulfilling choice for you. So put the stress and anxiety on the back burner and listen to your heart.

Chapter 3

Handling the Cost of College

What is a cynic? A man who knows the price of everything and the value of nothing.

—*Oscar Wilde*, Lady Windermere's Fan

It is impossible to make a system foolproof because fools are so ingenious.

—*Source Unknown*

Assuming that you and your parents begin the search for the right university in a systematic and coordinated way, there are certain house rules to be followed. We have developed these observations over the years based on personal interaction with hundreds of college applicants and their parents.

The average annual income of college graduates significantly exceeds that of non-graduates. The cost of a college education, therefore, should be looked on as an investment, not an expenditure. That is the mantra. The issue involves both getting the most value from your education and keeping its cost within reason.

THE COST: PUBLIC VERSUS PRIVATE

Typically, purchasers of higher education (usually, Mom and Dad) suffer from sticker shock when they calculate the annual tab for tuition, dormitory costs, and books. Naturally, the state-supported universities immediately appear to be the best buy. However, upon further review, this may not be true.

The tables that follow are not meant to suggest one option over the other but are intended to help students and their families compare possibilities. Each of the authors has three degrees and each has two from state-related universities. If we were to pose the question, "What do the Universities of Virginia, California (Berkley), and the College of William and Mary have in common?" the answer would be that they are three of the finest academic institutions and each is a state (public) school. Our purpose is to encourage readers to consider both public and private colleges in their journey to find the right school.

The table below compares costs and aid between a state and a private university in the 2006–2007 academic year, based on data from "Making The Case," a 2006 report by the Association of Independent Colleges and Universities of Pennsylvania (AICUP). To use this table, simply substitute the cost and the financial aid from the universities you are considering.

TABLE 3.1 Comparative Price Analysis Over Four Years		
	State University	Private University
Tuition, room, and board	$69,000	$160,000
Financial aid directly from the university in the form of renewable grants per year (not loans)	$18,000	$62,000
Total	$51,000	$98,000

Federal, state, or foundation monies and scholarships for athletics and academics are *not* included in the comparison on the assumption that these would be available at both state and private schools.

FOUR OR FIVE YEARS TO GRADUATE?

Although the state university is the cheaper option in the above scenario, it is important to remember that it often takes students in these institutions five years to earn a bachelor's degree. Private schools have a much higher four-year graduation rate. The primary reason for this is class availability. In the private schools, there are fewer students vying for a seat in the class. In many large universities, 1,500 students may need to take a class that has only 1,000 openings, and this may occur in multiple courses. Sometimes the required courses are not offered every semester. Consequentially, the student is compelled to spend an extra year in school to be able to take all of the necessary classes.

EARNINGS IN THE FIFTH YEAR

If you graduate in four years you not only save the cost of a fifth year in college, but you also gain the salary you earn in that year, assuming you begin working soon after graduation. This amount is a function of your field of study and general market conditions, but it is often substantial. According to Mary Jeanne Welsh, chairperson of LaSalle University's accounting department, the top 25 percent of 2007 graduates in LaSalle's accounting program had starting salaries averaging $54,000. The impact of this opportunity cost is shown in Table 3.2. We have considered only the fifth year in this scenario, but a year's start in the job market, or in graduate or professional school, usually provides a long-term advantage in pay increases and promotions as well.

TABLE 3.2 Comparative Price Analysis Over Five Years		
	State University	Private University
Tuition, room, and board (Four years)	$69,000	$160,000
University financial aid	($18,000)	($62,000)
Total	$51,000	$98,000
Cost of fifth year	$12,750	0
Income in fifth year	0	($54,000)
Net cash outflow over five years	$63,750	$44,000

Under these conditions, the private university is actually less expensive than the public one. Thus, in determining the relative costs of higher education, it is important to recognize that a fifth year of school involves not only extra tuition and fees but also a lost opportunity to earn a year's salary. Talk to some seniors during your campus visits to see how many of them actually graduate in four years. Graduation rates are reported by the schools annually to the Integrated Postsecondary Education Data System (IPEDS), and this information is available to the public. Various external organizations (*U.S. News & World Report* and the College Board, to name two) also report the information through annual surveys. Of course, the university that you are considering can also provide the information.

TABLE 3.3

1. Those who graduated in four years with a bachelor's degree by type of school

   - state universities   26%

   - state-related universities 35%

   - private universities   61%

2. Sources of financial aid to first-time freshmen in independent colleges (private)

   - state grants   7%

   - federal grants   7%

   - student loans   28%

   - institutional grants 59%

3. The state's investment in higher education for fiscal year 2004–2005

Sector	Percentage of Pennsylvania Total Dollars	Percentage of Pennsylvania Enrollment	Percentage of Pennsylvania Degrees
Private	15%	41%	49%
State-related	42%	24% (rounded)	26%
State	29%	17%	17%
Community colleges	14%	20%	8%

In December 2005, AICUP published a study in which every first year student enrolled in a four-year college in Pennsylvania was tracked. The study began in 1998 and was completed in June 2004. The reader is cautioned not to generalize. The study only looked at Pennsylvania. Some of the outcomes are presented in Table 3.3.

STRATEGIES TO REDUCE COSTS

There are a number of options to consider for lowering the cost of college.

Community or Junior Colleges

These schools are cheaper and consist of two-year programs in which the graduate receives an associate's degree. You may then be in a position to transfer to a four-year college to pursue a bachelor's degree. One caveat: It may require more than two years of course work at the senior institution to complete the degree requirements. The reason, typically, is because some of the completed courses are not transferable to the senior school.

This situation has been improved significantly in recent years by an agreement between many schools known as The Comprehensive Articulation Agreement. This contract defines and lists all the courses that have been categorized as transferable between the two schools involved. Essentially, junior college graduates retain all of their courses in the transfer process. The rationale is that sufficient commonality exists in the lower-division courses to develop a common general educational component. It is accepted that equivalent competencies have been developed in either school. Obviously, one must determine if the agreement exists with the admission offices of both colleges.

In-State Tuition

If you are considering an out-of-state university that has a lower tuition for in-state students, you may want to move to that state ahead of time. If you live there for a year, you usually become eligible for in-state tuition. Most states also require that you be financially self sufficient, that is, not a dependent of out-of-state parents.

For most families, this is not an attractive plan. In some circumstances, however, it is worth considering. In particular, your ability to find a suitable living arrangement and a job, or other constructive activity, is vital. Additionally, some state university systems have reciprocity agreements with neighboring states to grant in-state tuition to their residents. This may be a more feasible option to look into.

Advanced Placement (AP) Courses

College-level courses taken in high school could allow you to test out of some college classes. This may allow you to graduate early and save considerably on the cost. At the very least, you may be able to take additional courses of your choice, or electives, if the AP courses fulfill some of the university core requirements.

College-Level Examination Program (CLEP)

Most colleges offer CLEP exams to allow you to receive college credit. If you pass, these courses are waived and the potential to save significant amounts of money in tuition is a reality.

What is CLEP? The College Level Examination Program provides the opportunity to earn college credit for what you already know by achieving qualifying scores on any of the 34 CLEP examinations. According to the CLEP literature, approximately 3,000 colleges and universities accept your subject knowledge acquired through life experience, independent study, professional development, and internships. Typically, a certain minimum score on the exam can earn you from 3 to 12 college credits.

The test costs $65, and the university that accepts the CLEP results charge approximately $25 per credit. These costs are a fraction of the tuition and fees for the corresponding course in the classroom. The people who utilize CLEP most are older students who are attending school part time in the evening.

Summer Courses

College courses are usually less expensive in the summer. Consider taking a class or two during that time. You might also take classes at a less-expensive community college and transfer the credits to your home institution. This may allow you to graduate early or to take some of your courses at the part-time rate. Just be sure to check that your home university accepts credits from your community college.

Two-For-One

If you and a sibling attend the same college concurrently, you may be eligible for a significant reduction in the total tuition cost.

FINANCIAL AID

It is a given that the benefits of attending college are well worth the cost, but, for most families, paying for college will be a short-term financial emergency in which lifestyles will change during a period of belt-tightening. Parents whose first child is matriculating to college often see it as a horrific expense that they cannot afford. Here is the good news: Financial aid is available. Each school, especially in the private sector, has millions of dollars to help people meet the costs. Schools compete for students and the carrot is the financial aid package awarded to the applicant. Basically, colleges proclaim, "We will help you pay for your education." Some financial aid is based on student achievement, and some is determined, wholly or in part, by financial need.

The Meaning of Need-based Financial Aid

Financial need is:

> Total cost of college
>
> - Expected family contribution
> _____
> = Financial need

The federal government has established a standardized method of determining your financial need. You simply complete and file the Free Application for Federal Student Aid (FAFSA) form, which is available from high school guidance offices and public libraries.

The amount determined by the federal government is referred to as the Expected Family Contribution (EFC). It is based on income, assets, number of dependents, and other family members in college. Since EFC does not change from school to school, your financial need will vary with the cost of the college. It is important to note the total cost of a year at the university—including tuition, fees, room, board, and books—is often not listed in the award letters issued by the school. According to a 2007 article in *U.S. News & World Report*, the total cost in many schools is revealed only upon request because of a fear of driving applicants away.

SOURCES OF AID: GRANTS AND SCHOLARSHIPS

There are numerous sources for financial aid. Students and parents should explore as many as possible and pursue all those for which they are eligible.

Grants

Grants are based on need and do not have to be repaid. They are available at the federal and state levels and can be applied to the cost of the school of your choice. Universities provide grant money in addition to these government gifts. This is a crucial element in the decision to select one school over another. Among comparable schools, you want to get the best deal. How much money is the university giving you? How much will it cost after taking grants and scholarships into account?

Federal Pell Grants

If your EFC is below $4,200, you may receive a maximum possible Pell Grant, $4,310 for the 2007–2008 academic year. The amount of the grant is not flexible or subjectively determined. Rather, a chart comparing need with income tells you the amount of aid for which you qualify. The Pell Grant need not be repaid. Ninety percent of all

Pell Grants go to students whose families have incomes of less than about $40,000 a year (2007).

FSEOG Awards

Another source of grant money is Federal Supplemental Educational Opportunity Grants (FSEOG). If you are a Pell Grant recipient, you receive priority for FSEOG awards that range from $100 to $4,000 per year. Also, this grant does not have to be repaid. Earmarked for undergraduates with exceptional financial need, the funds depend on the availability of monies at the school. That means the school determines the amount, and it is not regulated by the federal government.

It is important to note that you must reapply for federal student aid every year. For more information and listings of financial aid resources, turn to the Appendix at the end of this book.

Scholarships

As a grant is a gift, so is a scholarship. It may cover most of your college cost or only a small portion of it. It usually requires you to maintain a certain level of academic performance (e.g., a B average) to have the scholarship renewed. Be aware that colleges like Pomona College in California and most Ivy League schools refuse to award scholarships based on good grades or test scores, according to the April 16, 2007, article "Run the Numbers" in *U.S. News & World Report*. Rather, these schools award scholarships as a function of financial need only.

Some scholarships are applicable to any university to which you have been accepted; others are offered by a specific university if you enroll there. There are many types of scholarships. For information on online sources where you can search for scholarships for which you may qualify, turn to the Appendix at the end of this book.

National Merit Scholarships

The National Merit Scholarship Program is an academic competition for recognition and scholarships. High school students enter the National Merit Program by taking the Preliminary SAT/National Merit Scholarship Qualifying Test (PSAT/NMSQT), which serves as an initial screen of approximately 1.3 million entrants each year, and by meeting published program entry/participation requirements.

To participate in the National Merit Scholarship Program, a student must take the PSAT/NMSQT in the specified year of the high school program and no later than the third year in grades 9 through 12.

Of the 1.3 million entrants, some 50,000 with the highest PSAT/NMSQT Index scores (critical reading + math + writing skills scores) qualify for recognition in the National Merit Scholarship Program. Students will fall into one of the following groups:

- Commended Students: In late September, more than two-thirds, or about 34,000 of the approximately 50,000 high scorers on the PSAT/NMSQT, receive Letters of Commendation in recognition of their outstanding academic promise. Although Commended Students do not continue in the competition for Merit Scholarship awards, some of these students do become candidates for Special Scholarships sponsored by corporations and businesses.

- Semifinalists: In early September, about 16,000 students, or approximately one-third of the 50,000 high scorers, are notified that they have qualified as semifinalists. To be considered for a Merit Scholarship award, semifinalists must advance to finalist standing in the competition by meeting high academic standards and other requirements.

- Winner Selection: All winners of Merit Scholarship awards are chosen from the Finalist group, based on their abilities, skills, and accomplishments.

Merit Scholarship awards are of three types. They are:

- National Merit $2,500 scholarships: Every finalist competes for these single payment scholarships, which are awarded on a state representational basis. To ensure that academically talented young people from every part of the United States are included in the competition, candidates are designated for a scholarship based on the highest scoring entrants in each state. Winners are selected without consideration of family financial circumstances, college choice, or major and career plans.

- Corporate-sponsored Merit Scholarship awards: Corporate sponsors designate their awards for children of their employees or members, for residents of a community where a company has operations, or for finalists with career plans the sponsor wishes to encourage. These scholarships may either be renewable for four years of undergraduate study or one-time awards.

- College-sponsored Merit Scholarship awards: Officials of each sponsor college select winners of their awards from finalists who have been accepted for admission. These awards are renewable for up to four years of undergraduate study.

Merit Scholarship awards are supported by some 500 independent sponsors and by the National Merit Scholarship Corporation's (NMSC) funds.

There are also special Merit Scholarships awarded each year. Some 1,500 National Merit Program participants who are not finalists are awarded Special Scholarships provided by corporations and business organizations. To be considered for a Special Scholarship, students must meet the sponsor's criteria and entry requirements of the National Merit Scholarship Program. They also must submit an entry form to the sponsor organization.

University Merit-Based Scholarships

Each year, most universities award merit-based scholarships to first-year and transfer students. Candidates are selected on such criteria as quality of high school course selection, grade point average (GPA), class rank, and standardized test scores.

Varying in amount from several thousand dollars to full tuition, university merit-based scholarships recognize academic excellence and extracurricular achievements. You may even qualify for more than one, in which case you would receive only the larger one.

Athletic Scholarships

Although the most well-known athletic scholarships are those awarded to star athletes in football and basketball, there are also full and partial scholarships at many colleges for lacrosse, wrestling, softball, hockey, team manager, trainer, cheerleader, and many other activities connected with athletics. Check to see if a scholarship is available for your activity or sport.

Community Service Scholarships

If you have participated in community service and demonstrated leadership in this work while in high school, you may be eligible for a scholarship at some universities.

University-Specific Scholarships

Many universities have scholarships available with criteria specific to that university. Some are also available for specific majors. Check with the financial aid officers for information on these.

Employee Scholarship and Discounts

Many colleges provide scholarships to the children of employees. Faculty and professional staff usually receive full tuition remission for their spouses and children. These scholarships are often applicable to a wide group of colleges in addition to the one where the family member is employed. Employees, other than faculty and professional staff, usually receive partial cost reductions. A parent who is in a position to change jobs might take a position at a college to be eligible for this kind of assistance. Students who plan to attend college on a part-time basis could obtain a job at a college and have their tuition paid.

Other types of employers may provide tuition assistance for employees and sometimes for their children as well.

Other Assistance

A wide variety of other sources of aid are available, including aid from foundations, corporations, unions, and fraternal organizations, including those specific to students who meet certain criteria, for example those who are members of certain ethnic or national groups, women over 25, and even surprising ones—such as for students who play the bagpipe, and so on.

Other programs include AmeriCorps and the U.S. Armed Forces, which offer financial aid opportunities in return for work in community service or in the military. You will find it helpful to check the FastWeb, CollegeNet, and CollegeBoard Web sites for sources of aid.

ROTC SCHOLARSHIPS AND VETERANS BENEFITS

Army Reserve Officer Training Corps (ROTC) scholarships are offered at hundreds of colleges. The Naval Reserve Officers Training Corps (NROTC) offers both two-year and four-year scholarships. The Air Force Reserve Officers Training Corps (AFROTC) college scholarship program focuses on students pursuing certain foreign language and technical degrees, but students studying in a wide variety of majors may be accepted into this program.

If a prospective student or his or her spouse is a veteran, educational benefits may be available. To be a recipient of scholarship aid, one must have been an active duty service member. The best strategy is to contact your local U.S. Department of Veterans Affairs office and the universities you are considering. For more information visit: http://www.gibill.va.gov.

TAX CREDITS

The Internal Revenue Service offers two federal income tax credits for higher education expenses. The Hope Tax Credit is worth up to $1,500 per student and is available for first- and second-year students. The other is the Lifetime Learning Tax Credit. It is a tax benefit equal to 20 percent of a family's tuition expenses, up to $10,000.

The Federal Income Tax Reduction Act (1997) allows for a tax credit for many middle-income families. This benefit provides eligible families up to $1,500 in federal tax credits per year. It is important to note that it is a credit not a *deduction* on your income tax return. The difference is that a credit reduces the amount of the tax directly, while a deduction reduces the amount of income that is subject to the tax. A tax deduction is subtracted from your adjusted gross income before you calculate your federal income tax owed. A tax credit entitles the taxpayer to subtract the amount of the credit (dollar-for-dollar) from the total federal income tax owed.

LOANS

Usually, financial aid will not cover all of your college costs. Only about half of the students receive grant or scholarship money in a given year, reports *U.S. News & World Report*. The truth, as noted in "New Math for College Costs" in the March 13, 2006, issue of *Newsweek*, is that thousands of dollars of loans are needed to fill the deficit after scholarships, savings, and earnings are utilized.

Because of rising costs, students may borrow more via government-backed loans. More than 60 percent of four-year undergraduates finance their education with debt accumulation. On average, the graduates leave school with $15,000 to $20,000 in debt to the government. The good news is that there is no evidence that these debts prevent students from marrying, buying a home, or living independently, according to the American Council on Education.

At the federal level, there are two low-interest loan programs, Perkins and Stafford, to assist college students. In 2007, Perkins is the federal government's lowest-cost student loan. Your school will decide how much you qualify for, but no student can borrow more than $4,000 a year. Needy students may qualify for both loans. There is a grace period of at least six months after graduation before you have to begin payments on these loans. The logic to this approach is that six months after graduation you will be employed in a well-paying job. If you go on to graduate or professional school, you can postpone payment while enrolled in such programs. For graduates working in some types of public service professions such as teaching, health care, and social work, all or part of the loan may be forgiven. There are a growing number of programs that forgive.

Do not automatically accept the lender recommended by the university. You may be able to make more suitable arrangements with a different lender.

Perkins Loans

Perkins loans are federal loans that have a fixed interest rate of 5 percent for a maximum of $4,000 for undergraduates. The average Perkins loan was $1,998 in 2007. The average may not be the amount you receive.

Payment is owed to the school that made the loan. There is no minimum award amount. These loans are also available for graduate students, with a $6,000 maximum.

Perkins loans are awarded only to students who are found to be very needy and have very low Expected Family Contributions (EFC).

Stafford Loans (Subsidized)

Stafford loans are the most popular federally guaranteed loans. Effective fall 2007, the interest rate is 6.8 percent. Under the rubric of subsidized loans, there are two categories for this federally funded vehicle: Subsidized FFEL or Direct Stafford Loan. The former, FFEL, is the Federal Family Education Loan. The latter is from the William D. Ford Federal Direct Loan Program. In either case, the loan must be repaid and you must be at least a half-time student. The connotation of "subsidized" refers to the fact that the interest is paid by the U.S. Department of Education while the student is in school and during grace and deferment periods. The annual award amounts range from $3,500 to $7,500 in the first year but can be higher in the second, third, and fourth year (2007), determined by the government's evaluation of need. The interest rate on the loan changes yearly.

Stafford Loans (Unsubsidized)

The difference between subsidized and unsubsidized is the payment of interest. With an unsubsidized loan, the borrower is responsible for the interest during the life of the loan. Financial need is not a requirement and the award amounts are the same.

PLUS Loans (FFEL or Direct PLUS Loans)

These loans are available to parents of dependent undergraduate students enrolled at least half-time. The maximum amount is *cost of attendance* (see glossary later in this chapter) minus any other financial aid the student receives. There is no minimum award amount; the loan must be repaid, and the interest rate is 8.85 percent for 10-year loans beginning in the fall of 2007.

Whether you receive a Direct or a FFEL loan depends on which program the school you attend participates in. For a comprehensive presentation relative to grants and loans from the U.S. Department of Education, there are two primary sources: http://studentaid.ed.gov and 1-800-4-FED-Aid (1-800-433-3243).

If your parents have a good credit rating, they may be in a position to borrow the full net or out-of-pocket cost of each child's annual college expense through the federal PLUS program (2007).

Home Equity Loans

Something to consider by parents with significant home equity is a home equity loan at 7 percent. The rationale for this type of loan for families earning more than $135,000 is that the educational debt is not tax deductible, but the higher mortgage payments are, and these payments would reduce the amount owed to the IRS by several hundred dollars a year.

Parents should not borrow from their 401(k)s! A home equity loan is a better option if federal loans do not generate enough cash. If you have insignificant equity in your home, parents would be better served by a Plus loan. Plus loans offer forgiveness of the loan if the parent becomes disabled. If either the student or the parent dies, forgiveness kicks in. Lastly, as with Perkins and Stafford loans, there are federal programs to reduce some education loans if the student majors in such programs as nursing, education, or social work, or takes a federal position in certain skill areas.

There are also financial strategies to reduce your repayment costs. If as a student, graduate, or parent you have at least one federally backed educational loan, you may be able to lock in the current rate before it changes, or consolidate the debt. By doing so, you get a fixed rate at whatever the current rate is. In 2007, the federal government made PLUS loans directly to the parents at an annual percentage rate (APR) of 8.85 on a 10-year loan. Financial aid officers recommend shopping for the best deal. Many lenders provide incentives such as a reduction of a quarter of a point off the interest rate if you agree to pay by automatic debit. To seek the best consolidation offer, check with the school's financial aid office. Presently, Stafford loans are the best value at 6.8 percent. This ratio is fixed, meaning that it is not subject to change.

WORK

Most schools have a program that provides you with an opportunity to earn a fixed amount per year through a variety of campus jobs. When the maximum is reached, the job becomes available to another student. This Work-Study Program is designed to provide you with spending money, rather than reduce tuition. Typically, you can work up to 15 hours per week, and receive a biweekly paycheck.

You might, instead, consider an off-campus job. These often pay much more than work-study jobs. Depending on the nature of the job and the hours, it may provide a valuable supplemental experience to college classes, or it may detract from the time and energy needed to excel in college.

SAVINGS

From a parental perspective, the cost of college for your child is second only to the purchase of a home in terms of total cost outlay.

What amount of savings must be systematically invested? The answer is a function of how much the savings/investments will earn over the projected period. An educated guess is the best answer you can hope for when facing these problems.

If your son or daughter were planning to attend a private college in 2007–2008 the *average* annual cost of tuition, fees, room, and board was $40,000.

However, if the cost continues to increase at a rate of 6 percent per annum, in the 2011–2012 academic year the estimated cost is $50,500. A four-year education, beginning in the fall of 2007 would cost approximately $175,000 (list price before grants, loans, and so on). For young families, cost projections of this type can lead to the most extreme form of panic.

There is good news! According to The College Board's Trends in College Pricing 2006–2007, 74 percent of undergraduate students received financial aid and the federal and state governments awarded more than $130 billion in grants. Ultimately, the major issue is determining how much you need to save. Assuming a systematic savings plan is implemented and assuming a savings growth rate of 6 percent, the following table, adapted from New York Life's Summer 2005 Intouch Newsletter, is a guideline.

Table 3.4

Save Per Month	5 years	10 years	18 Years
$50	$3,109	$6,454	$12,339
$100	$6,219	$12,909	$24,678
$250	$15,549	$32,273	$61,696
$500	$31,099	$64,546	$123,392
$1,000	$62,199	$129,093	$246,785

This example assumes a 25 percent federal tax rate on the annual earnings and a 3 percent inflation rate.

What can be learned from these data? Unequivocally, the earlier you begin to save, the better. Many parents postpone educational savings for present-day purchases, but in doing so they fail to capitalize on the magic of compound interest. Simply put, the longer the period of compounding, the greater is the reward. Conclusion: The key to successful planning for college is to begin saving as early, and as much, as possible! And take advantage of tax breaks on money being saved for college.

Savings and Tax Plans

If you consult a financial planner or a tax accountant, you may uncover ways in which the family can save money on college expenses, such as having the son or daughter declare financial independence, or perhaps having the parents file separate tax returns and only one taking the child as a dependent. The best strategy to use, of course, varies with such factors as family income and the parents' marital status. This is also true in determining the best savings plan to use. A couple of examples are Educational and Savings Accounts (ESAs) and 529 College Savings Plans.

Educational and Savings Accounts are savings plans that provide parents, grandparents, and students the opportunity to contribute up to $2,000 per year (until the student turns 18) toward qualified education expenses at any college or university. Known as Coverdells, ESAs are designed to encourage long-term saving by allowing the investment vehicle to be tax-deferred during the investment growth period and withdrawals to be tax-free when the proceeds are used for educational expenses. There are income limits that prevent some from participating. The adjusted gross income parameters are up to $220,000 for married taxpayers and $110,000 for single taxpayers.

529 College Savings Plans are state-sponsored accounts that allow families to save college money in a tax-deferred investment vehicle. Money can be withdrawn tax free from a 529 when it is used for paying for college. Originally set to expire in 2010, the

federal government in 2006 made this perk permanent. As a result, 529 assets are increasing exponentially—from $68.4 billion to $90.7 billion in one year. Furthermore, 529 plan fees are decreasing. California's direct-sold 529 includes a low-cost index fund that charges 0.5 percent in annual management fees.

Contributions in most 529 plans grow entirely tax-free, ergo no capital gains hassle. A capital gains tax is a federal tax on profits derived from capital assets as in property, stocks, bonds, etc. Anyone can contribute, whether the plan is for your child, sibling, or family friend. There are two types, prepaid and savings. The prepaid plan is a contract that locks in the current tuition rate. Only 14.8 percent of the 529 plans are prepaid. Typically, parents may utilize the prepaid plan a year before the student enrolls. Rarely, if ever, does one select the plan prior to this time.

The savings plan consists of mutual funds that grow tax-free. In either type of 529, one can invest in excess of $300,000 per beneficiary. Many well-known fund managers such as Merrill Lynch and Fidelity, among many others, are the vehicles to use in creating a 529 savings account. It is important to note that plan costs range from 0 to 2.5 percent of your assets per year plus sales fees of your purchase plans through brokers.

In March 2006, the Municipal Securities Rulemaking Board, which regulates 529s, mandated that investment firms are required to tell clients that their home-state plan may offer tax breaks, and that going out of state may cost a tax deduction. To expedite the new rule, the College Savings Plans Network functions as an information conduit on state-run college savings plans. The CSPN provides comparative data on competing 529s. Parents can research and compare this information online at: http://www .collegesavings.org and http://savingforcollege.com. This allows parents to develop a strategy to cope with the projected rising costs of college.

It is best *not* to put college savings in the student's name. This is likely to reduce financial aid.

STEPS IN APPLYING FOR AID

The process of applying for aid is relatively simple. There is no need to pay someone to do it for you, even though some companies solicit your money with exaggerated claims of how much they can do for you and how much aid they can secure for you. Often they simply provide Web sites to financial aid programs. Some even guarantee $2,625 in aid—the Stafford loan amount that every freshman is eligible to receive!

Fill Out the Application

You may fail to apply for aid because you believe you won't qualify. Not only does this prevent you from receiving need-based aid if you are, in fact, eligible, it also removes federal loans as a possibility. All that you are required to do is complete the Free Application for Federal Student Aid (FAFSA). In essence, you are asked about family income, savings, and other assets, to determine how much you should be expected to pay for college costs, known as Expected Family Contribution (EFC).

Your high school guidance counselor can provide the FAFSA document or call 1-800-4-FED-AID. Submit the FAFSA after January 1.

Submit the Application on Time

Frequently, applicants wait until after their acceptance letters come before applying for aid. This is too late. Aid is a function of many sources and each has different deadline dates. Typically, they are between March 1 and June 30. Since aid is generally awarded on a first-come, first-served basis, you should apply early before the bulk of the awards have been made.

About four weeks after mailing the form, you should receive the Student Aid Report (SAR) from the U.S. Department of Education. The SAR will define exactly your EFC. Mail the SAR to the colleges you are hoping to attend.

COMPARING FINANCIAL AID PACKAGES

Congratulations! You have been accepted by several colleges. Now the real financial analysis begins. Rarely are two schools' financial aid packages identical, even though they may appear to be. What, at first glance, appears to be the best offer, may be misleading.

Each college includes a detailed aid package with your acceptance letter. It consists of:

1. Grants and scholarships

2. Loans

3. Work-study packages

Grants and Scholarships

Analyze each school's "expected cost to attend," subtract grant and scholarship monies, and you have the actual cost of enrollment. This enables you to know your true out-of-pocket costs.

Some schools include loans and work-study earnings as part of the financial aid package that may then total 100 percent on the summary page. In this case, however, the largest aid package may be the one that generates the largest amount of personal debt. You must look beyond the summary page. Analyzing only this information could cost you thousands of dollars.

Remember that the schools have various marketing strategies for recruiting freshmen. A school with low tuition may only offer loans, whereas a school with an inflated sticker price often provides scholarships and grants.

The school's cost of attendance is also subject to interpretation. Some colleges list a number that is unrealistically low. Some include books, transportation, personal expenses, tuition, fees (watch out for this one), and room and board. If one school does not include all of the above in its definition of cost of attendance and another does, you are not comparing apples to apples. That which is not included would have to be added to your family contribution in order to accurately compare the packages. Here are a few additional points to keep in mind:

1. If you are awarded a scholarship, find out what is required to have it renewed for subsequent years. In the fine print, you may discover that you must maintain a high grade point average. If so, ask what percentage of upper class students retains their awards.

2. Don't assume that because a college has a higher tuition and gives a higher award, it is a better choice. Make the decision on which is a better place for you based on procedures we recommend in Chapter 5.

3. Remember to take into account whether it normally takes four or five years to graduate from this university.

4. Determine how many hours a week you could work without jeopardizing your studies.

5. Search for scholarships with late deadlines.

Loans

In comparing loans among schools, check out the effective interest rate. Some debt is costlier than others. Some loans accrue interest while you are in college, whereas with others, such as Stafford loans, interest commences six months after graduation. Some lenders offer a lower interest rate, but only if you meet the due date. Miss once and you forfeit the discounted rate.

Don't readily accept a Plus loan in the university's award package. The interest rate can be as high as 8 percent. You may be able to lower that interest rate with a home equity loan. The self-help part of the package consists of subsidized loans (Stafford loans) and university work-study jobs. But—and this is important— other loans are sometimes offered that are unsubsidized. Any student or parent can obtain these loans, which are not related to need-based aid, although the interest rate may be lower than some private loans.

Work

You may be offered a work-study job on the campus as a part of the financial aid award. Note how many hours per week the amount of money listed assumes and whether this is a reasonable commitment in terms of your other responsibilities. For example, if you also have a scholarship, will your work jeopardize your ability to meet the standards needed to retain it?

It Never Hurts to Ask

When the financial aid letter arrives, the amount may be less than you anticipated. What do you do? According to Kenneth Redd, director at the National Association of Student Financial Aid Administrators, the students or their parents should call or visit the aid office at the university to seek an appeal. If the amount is insufficient, Redd states that most financial aid offices will consider reviewing the package initially offered. This may be more negotiable if other schools have tendered a larger aid package. If you provide evidence to support your position, the possibility of more aid is increased. Maybe you failed to include some circumstances that would have generated a greater amount of aid. If a sibling has decided to return to college, creating a new financial hurdle for your parents, this would be an important point to mention. Some universities, such as Carnegie Mellon University and Harvard University, ask students to give them a chance to match other schools' financial aid packages.

Joe Paul Case, financial aid director at Amherst College, states, "You need to provide a narrative. We translate that narrative into dollars." For example, if your family has disproportionately high medical expenses, you would be in a position to receive special consideration.

A substantive and well-thought-out appeal, including documentation, is most effective. University officials are more responsive to inquiries that are polite and informative. If they perceive that you are genuinely seeking alternative ways of being able to attend their university, including your willingness to take on extra loans, your chances are significantly improved.

Generally, if contact is made in person (after making an appointment) the chances of winning your appeal are greater. The worst-case scenario is that your aid package remains unchanged.

On a more positive note, please remember, the financial aid office is there to help you come to their university.

A GLOSSARY OF FINANCIAL AID TERMS

As you correspond with the people in the financial aid office of any school, you will encounter financial aid terminology that might be unfamiliar to you. Listed below are some definitions.

award letter: An official document issued by a school's financial aid office itemizing all of the financial aid offered to the student.

costs of attendance: The total of tuition, fees, room, board, books, supplies, transportation, loan fees, and miscellaneous expenses.

direct loans: A federal loan program in which the school becomes the lending agency and manages the funds directly while the federal government provides the funds.

Expected Family Contribution (EFC): The amount the family is expected to contribute toward the student's education as determined by income, assets, family size, and the number of children in college concurrently.

Federal Family Education Loan Program (FFELP): Includes the Stafford Loan, the Perkins Loan, and the Parent Loan for Undergraduate Students (PLUS). Funds are provided by private lenders (banks), and the federal government guarantees against default. Families are encouraged to pursue companies and nonprofits for the best loan deals.

Federal Direct Student Loan Program (FDSLP): Similar to FFELP, but funds are distributed by the U.S. government directly to students and parents through their schools.

financial aid package: The total amount of financial aid offered by the school to the applicant.

Free Application for Federal Student Aid (FAFSA): Form that must be completed for all need-based aid such as grants, loans, and work-study jobs. No fee is charged to file a FAFSA.

(continues)

(continued)

Pell Grant: A federal grant that supplies funds up to $4,310 for the 2007-08 academic year.

Perkins loans: Loans that have a fixed interest rate of 5 percent for a maximum of $4,000 for undergraduates.

PLUS loans: Parents can borrow up to the entire cost of attendance less any other aid.

Stafford loans: The most popular federally guaranteed loans. Effective August 1, 2007, the rate is 6.8 percent. They come in two forms, subsidized and unsubsidized. The former is based on need; the latter is not.

Student Aid Report (SAR): This document calculates the difference between FAFSA and EFC. You should receive a copy of your SAR four to six weeks after you file your FAFSA.

subsidized loans: Loans for which the U.S. government pays interest while the student is in school.

Supplemental Educational Opportunity Grants: Pell Grant recipients receive priority for SEOG awards that range from $100 to $4,000 per year.

unmet need: The difference between a school's total cost of attendance and the sum of the family's EFC and its aid award.

unsubsidized loan: A loan for which the government does not pay the interest. The interest accrues while the student is in school but payment can be deferred until graduation.

work-study: Part-time jobs on campus that are federally funded.

SUMMARY

Higher education continues to get more expensive. The issue on the table is whether the cost of college will prevent lower- and middle-income students from pursuing a college education. Professor James

Heckman, a member of the faculty at the University of Chicago and a winner of the Nobel Prize in economics, states unequivocally: "No!" He finds that economically lower- and middle-income students enroll at almost the same rate as those from the highest-income families. Students from all economic levels can and do go to college!

Professors Paul Umbach and George Kuh state in the *Journal of Higher Education* that compelling arguments are being made that economic diversity among students benefits individual students, schools, and society as a whole. Specifically, diversity enhances the college experience of all students.

Chapter 4

Picking a Major and Planning a Career

Success is not the key to happiness, happiness is the key to success.

—*Albert Schweitzer*

Blessed is he who has found his work; let him ask no other blessedness.

—*Thomas Carlyle,* Past and Present

Although the value of a college education extends well beyond its role in helping you prepare for a career, that is one of the major advantages of attending college. Most well-paying, professional jobs today require a college degree. The career you choose is much more than a way of earning a living. A great deal of the satisfaction you get in life comes from the kind of work you do: your sense of accomplishment, your ability to seek challenging goals, the people you work with, and the feeling of being involved in something you value. Don't simply drift into a particular occupation. Spend some time and effort learning about the wide variety of career choices that are available and how your talents and interests match up with them.

In exploring possible careers, two resources are particularly helpful. *The Occupational Outlook Handbook*, published by the U.S. Department of Labor, includes a wealth of information on future trends in the job market, salary ranges, duties, and credentials for a large number of jobs. The World of Work Map is a self-assessment tool that groups college majors and careers into different categories. Using this map, it is possible to see which occupations are compatible with your interests. You can also relate various college majors to job families and careers.

Two additional aids are the Strong Interest Inventory and the Self-Directed Search, which are both self-assessment tests. In addition, guidance counselors can assist you in selecting and using these aids, and also in interpreting their results for your college planning.

DIFFICULTIES IN SELECTING A CAREER

You probably have only a vague idea of what most careers involve. Even if you are familiar with an occupation, you may not see the forest but only some of the trees. In the case of teaching, for example, you see only the work the teacher does in class and are unaware of the many other activities and requirements of that profession. Too often, information about careers is mainly obtained by watching television shows where neurosurgeons, forensic psychologists, crime reporters, and others are depicted in unrealistic and glamorized versions of these jobs. To get a more accurate picture, attend career fairs and consult current occupational information available in books and pamphlets and on Web pages.

At the same time, you probably do not know your current abilities, interests, and other traits very well, let alone what you will be like in the future. The college years are a period of self-exploration and development, so you should be better able to make career choices later in college than when you first enroll. Thus, you shouldn't expect to make a sure and sudden career decision as a high school senior or college freshman. Rather, this choice should be made as a gradual developmental process, in which you test yourself against a number of challenges, explore new territory, and learn more about the world, including the work world.

An early step in the process is picking a major when you first start college. It helps to prioritize what the major means to you. A career-focused major makes the postgraduate job search easier, or, at least, more specific. But, "easier" should not be part of the criteria. Don't give up on the opportunity to broaden your knowledge and skills so you can focus on a major that is, in all likelihood, not your life's work. An informal study of accounting graduates by Dr. Reardon in the 1980s found about half of them working in positions unrelated to accounting five years after graduation.

Some careers obviously require a specific major (computer science, electrical engineering); others do not. You can qualify for law school with almost any undergraduate major. Education majors can pursue a Master of Business Administration (MBA) and leave the teaching profession. Still, you are usually better off picking a major right at the start, even if you subsequently change it. Many colleges do not require students to declare a major until sophomore year.

SOURCES OF ASSISTANCE

Your main sources of assistance in this process are parents, other family members, high school teachers, and guidance counselors. In addition, it is natural to discuss career possibilities with friends. Ultimately, however, you must take responsibility for your own life. So get what assistance you can in the decision-making process, but make your own decisions.

A TENTATIVE MAJOR

Usually the choice of a major is a tentative one. As you learn more about the demands of the major and other opportunities available, you may decide to change your major (a high percentage of students do, sometimes several times). Most students, in fact, change their major at least once during their undergraduate years. And those who change majors are sometimes more satisfied than those who stay with their initial choice. You and your parents should not interpret a change of major as a failure or weakness. It is, rather, a normal part of the developmental process for many young people.

It is possible to register as "undecided" if you are uncertain about your major, but we believe this is a mistake. Students who select a major, even one they subsequently change, have a goal, even if it is tentative, that will help give focus to their work and may improve their academic performance.

You should plan your classes so that you can get a sample of at least one course in your prospective major at an early stage. Most of the courses in the first year are part of the core curriculum that can apply to any major. As valuable in your liberal education as these core courses are, it is also of enormous practical help to find out early if your chosen or preferred major is not right for you. Should this turn out to be the case, you are usually able to make the change to another major and still graduate in four years. Should you wait until your junior year to decide on a major, and then want to change, it is likely that you will have to attend for a fifth year to complete the requirements. If you don't like your major, don't stick it out, hoping that things will get better. They won't. You've got to be interested in what you are learning.

Aside from taking a course in a subject, there are other ways to explore a major. Read a textbook, speak with faculty members and students from the department, and peruse occupational information to learn more about the major requirements and the careers it prepares you to pursue. See if you can acquire work experience, either paid or as a volunteer or intern, that is related to your career plans.

If you are having difficulty deciding on a major, it helps to select a college that has resources to provide the assistance you need. At a minimum, this would include excellent career counseling services and the opportunity to explore a variety of subjects in your course selections.

CAREER CHOICE AND MAJOR

In choosing a major, even a tentative one, you must consider the quality of that department at your prospective colleges and not just the general quality of the schools. This may seem obvious, but we have met students who picked a college because of its general appeal without realizing that it did not offer the major they wanted, or that the department in which they planned to major had serious limitations. At one college, a student who wants chemical engineering may have to major in chemistry instead, or at another the demands may be unrealistically high so that 90 percent of the students in that major fail in their first year. In other cases, the department may be so small that one or two faculty members teach all of the courses in the discipline, limiting a student's chance to experience a variety of viewpoints. In a large university, by contrast, a department may have a strong reputation in science because of its graduate programs, but its undergraduate courses may be far too large for effective teaching, or the courses may be taught by graduate assistants rather than the faculty who are the basis for the university's reputation. In still other cases, a department may emphasize aspects of the major that differ from a student's interest. For example, you may have an interest in clinical or counseling psychology, but wind up in a program that emphasizes animal learning or neuropsychological research.

When visiting a college, make sure you meet with students and faculty in the department in which you plan to major. Check to see if the department has appropriate equipment and facilities. Ask the students about the classes, the teaching quality, and the general spirit of the department. In some departments you may find that there is considerable conflict and dissatisfaction, whereas in others there is enthusiasm and a positive attitude.

Other questions to ask include how long it typically takes to graduate in your prospective major (four or five years) and about the track record of the department's graduates in obtaining jobs or admission to graduate or professional schools. In a surprising number of cases, it takes the average student five years to complete the bachelor's program. By contrast, some colleges have programs that enable a student to get both a BA and an MA in five years. This is worth considering if you are sure that you want a master's degree in that subject.

CHANGING MAJORS

Even if you are confident in your choice of a major, it is worth checking on the ease of transferring to another major, since many students, in fact, do make at least one change. For example, an informal university study done by the admissions department at LaSalle University discovered that, on average, 2 out of 3 students changed their major at least

DUAL MAJORS AND MINORS

In many cases, it is possible to have dual majors (for example, history and political science or biology and chemistry). More commonly, students take a minor (or perhaps more than one) in addition to their major. Some minors, like modern languages, science, or business, improve your chances for success on the job; others, like art, music, or English literature, broaden your education and provide sources for enjoyment.

once. In some colleges, changing a major may require a year or more of additional courses; in others it may be done with little difficulty.

Another consideration is that some related careers have very different types of training. For example, mental health professionals include psychiatrists, clinical and counseling psychologists, professional counselors, marriage and family therapists, social workers, and psychiatric nurses. To become a psychiatrist you must take a program of undergraduate studies that will prepare you for medical school. The most common undergraduate majors for this are biology and chemistry, but if you are also considering becoming a psychologist, you would be better off to have a major, or at least a minor, in psychology in case you decide that you would rather become a clinical psychologist instead of a psychiatrist.

THE VALUE OF A LIBERAL ARTS EDUCATION

The maturation and learning that occurs during the college years is valuable for any career. A liberal arts education helps you develop a better understanding of yourself and your world. Characteristics of a well-educated individual include the ability to organize resources, accomplish projects, communicate orally and in writing in a manner that is informative and persuasive, and the ability to set priorities and critically seek and evaluate both qualitative and quantitative information. These qualifications are valuable in all aspects of life, including selecting a career, becoming successful in it, and finding satisfaction in it.

Clearly, it is important to have a balance between courses related to your major and those intended for your general intellectual and emotional development. High school students looking at a college's curriculum may wonder why there isn't more immediate focus on courses in their major. Some say, "Why do I have to take all of this other junk?" This "other junk" provides some of the most valuable experience in helping the student become a well-educated person.

DOS AND DON'TS FOR FAMILY

Parents and other family members can play a significant role in helping students make wise choices in career planning and selecting a major. Here are some recommendations for them.

What to Do

1. Be involved and informed. Although students should play a major role in decisions that affect their lives, at this stage in their development, they usually require help. Families should aim not only at the goal of guiding students to make a wise choice, but also in enabling them to become better qualified at making future decisions on their own.

2. Be supportive. Students are often under considerable pressure over the whole process of finding the right college, selecting a major and potential career, and getting accepted into the college of their choice. Moreover, they often go about the selection process in ways that you and other adults see as far from optimal. As a parent, it is natural to feel like grabbing your teen by the shoulders and talking some sense into them, however, it is better to pat them on the back and be encouraging.

3. Help students to recognize their talents. Young people often are overly aware of their limitations yet take their strengths for granted. As a parent you probably know your teen well enough to help him or her make more realistic self-assessments.

4. Learn along with them. No matter how much experience you as a parent have had with your own college choices or with college choices made by other family members, you will find that there is much you are unaware of about careers and college majors when it comes time for your teen to make these choices. You can set a good example by the way you go about obtaining this information and sharing it with other family members who are involved in the college-planning process.

Family members can also help by encouraging students to explore opportunities and challenges in planning for their future. This includes obtaining a liberal arts education that will prepare them for more in life than a career.

What Not to Do

1. Limit career choices. A common mistake family members make is to emphasize one or a few career choices. We remember a parent who said his son could choose whichever career he wanted. "Either a doctor or a lawyer," he said, "it's up to him." Often, when the parents pressure a student to pursue a major, the student will passively go along with the choice but with little personal interest and little effort. The end result is usually low grades, even failing ones.

2. Relive your own lives. Parents sometimes seek to relive their own lives through their child, often to the detriment of the child's development. Thus the father whose own college days were a grind of study and outside work and who regrets missing the social side of college, may overemphasize that aspect to his son. "Enjoy life when you are young," is his advice, "and get involved in as many activities as you can." Another parent, who paid her own way through college, may expect her daughter to do the same thing under different circumstances. "It was a good lesson for me, and it will be a good lesson for you."

3. Take on the student's responsibility. Taking over the student's responsibility is an easy mistake to make. Since the parents

want the best for their child, they sometimes gather the information themselves, talk to college admissions officers, determine which college their son or daughter should attend, and what he or she should select for a major. In doing this, they prevent the maturing adolescent from learning to make decisions about his or her life, something that is a necessary part of the maturation process.

4. Expecting too much from the student. At the other extreme, some parents expect their daughter or son to be able to negotiate this transition from high school to college with little or no help. We know better today than to teach children to swim by throwing them in the deep water. True, they must get in the water to learn to swim, but they need support and instruction, as well as other forms of assistance. In the same way, students must be involved in the college-selection process, but they need assistance and encouragement. Striking a balance between dominating the process and being indifferent to it is the key for parents.

CAREER COUNSELORS

Career counselors are another valuable source of help. They are trained to assist you in making educational and vocational plans, and you should take advantage of this service. If the student already has a career goal in mind, it might be helpful to meet with a career counselor to understand how this career goal can be met. Keep in mind, however, that career counseling is best undertaken at several points over a lifetime. Career counseling, like career planning, is a gradual process. One key time is when you are making the transition from high school to college.

HIGH SCHOOL COUNSELORS

In the best-case scenario, counselors assist you in better understanding your abilities, interests, and personality traits, and encourage you to explore information about careers that are consistent with your strengths. Unfortunately, schools vary widely in the kind of guidance counseling they provide. Some schools have too few counselors, so they are forced to limit their services; other schools may have some counselors who are ineffective. Thus, what can be an excellent resource for you is not consistently so. You and your parents need to evaluate the quality of the counseling services available in your school in deciding how much benefit they may be for you, or if you would be better served by making an appointment with a private counselor.

PRIVATE PROFESSIONAL COUNSELORS

When high schools have enough well-qualified counselors to provide individual services to all kinds of students, consulting a private practitioner is usually unnecessary. When schools lack adequate resources, however, this type of assistance can be invaluable. Of course, they too vary in quality of services they provide. One of Dr. Rooney's high school experiences with career counseling demonstrates why it's good to be skeptical. After taking a variety of tests, he met with the counselor who said, "Engineering is the field for you." Although he had considered engineering as a possibility, he was looking in other directions as well. It soon became clear that the counselor was focusing on certain parts of the test results and minimizing others. When asked about this, the counselor replied, "Do you know how much money engineers make?" Young Rooney decided that he should take this counselor's advice with a grain of salt.

The greatest value of career counseling is not so much in steering you away from careers that are inconsistent with your interests and talents (although this does happen), but in alerting you to careers that you haven't thought about that seem worth considering. Clearly, the counselor cannot decide for you, but he or she can be a dependable resource in the exploration process.

Students and parents who want a private practitioner for assistance in career choice should seek a counseling psychologist or a licensed professional counselor. Look for someone with a sound reputation who specializes in career counseling and has considerable experience working with high school students. This kind of service is well worth the cost. Professional associations of counselors or psychologists and university counseling centers can usually recommend a well-qualified career counselor.

COLLEGE COUNSELORS

Most colleges offer professional counseling services. Usually they are of high quality and include educational and career counseling, but some otherwise sound colleges neglect or minimize this invaluable resource. Look into the quality of such services in colleges you are considering, and utilize the counseling resources of the college you decide to attend.

PREDICTING THE FUTURE

One of the new developments demonstrated at the New York World's Fair in 1939 was television. In discussing whether TV would provide jobs in the future, the *New York Times* reviewer was skeptical. "The trouble with television," he wrote, "is that people must sit and keep their eyes glued on a screen; the average American family hasn't time for that." Other similar attempts to predict the future have demonstrated how difficult it is. Yet we can predict with confidence that there will be opportunities in the future that we are not aware of now, and that a broad education will help you prepare for them.

Whatever major you choose, it should serve as a base to use while exploring new territory. Careers of the future often lay in an area in which two disciplines overlap or where the methodology of one discipline can be applied in another. Exposure to new subjects opens new horizons that may be the basis for new perspectives on career choice. If you initially decide on a major in accounting, you may become intrigued with a course in economics and either switch majors or decide to combine the two interests. If you have an interest in science, but enjoy interacting with people much more than spending time in the laboratory, you may find a career in teaching science, pharmaceutical sales, or in administration.

People are also adaptable. You could, no doubt, be happy and successful in several different careers, so it is not a case of deciding on the one perfect choice, but of selecting one of several that would be suitable and avoiding ones that would be unsuitable for you.

Many graduates move into careers that are unrelated to their major. Education majors go on for an MBA, or to graduate work in sociology or psychology; political science majors go to law school, or become teachers; nurses become counselors.

A recent news story featured the wedding of two students who had met at college. It mentioned that she had become a pastry chef and loved it; he had always wanted to become a policeman and was looking forward to joining the police force. Neither of their majors was directly related to the work they were doing, but their education should help them have a more satisfying life and advance in their jobs.

Not all interests are satisfied through the job. As important as the work you do is for your well-being, hobbies, civic and community activity, and, of course, family, are all significant parts of your life. A person who loves music need not become a professional musician. A hobby or a sideline in music may be more practical. Many a budding musician, actor, writer, and artist have been advised: "Don't quit your day job," at least not until you have become successful enough at your hobby to do it as a full-time job.

SUMMARY

All of this advice about choosing a major can be simplified if you embrace one rule: Listen to your heart. Many young people focus on where the money is, but if you don't like your work, no amount of money will fulfill you. Follow your dream, not the bucks.

If you focus primarily on financial rewards, it can lead to a feeling of being incomplete and unfulfilled. Satisfaction comes from pursuing a goal that has significance. Your career must have purpose and passion, as well as profit.

When you love what you are doing, and know that you are doing something worthwhile, it is not work; it is happiness.

Chapter 5

The Right College,
Not the Best College

Out of clutter, find simplicity; from discord, find harmony; in the middle of difficulty, lies opportunity.

— *Albert Einstein*

There has been lots of progress during my lifetime, but I'm afraid it's heading in the wrong direction.

— *Ogden Nash*

A group of graduates from the same academically strong high school gathered at an informal reunion during the Thanksgiving break of their first year of college. Several of them, enrolled in prestigious universities, were grousing about the huge size of classes and the graduate assistants who were doing most of the teaching. Then a student, who had enrolled in a less-well-known four-year private college, spoke out. "That hasn't been my experience at all. Most of my classes have about 25 students. And one seminar has only 15. I have the chair of the English department for one class and enthusiastic teachers for all of them. It's a bit demanding, but it looks like I found the right college for me."

THE STEAK OR THE SIZZLE

Some schools appeal to the typical 18-year-old for the wrong reasons. Often, a winning football or basketball team will be the catalyst for the young person to seek admission to that university. This is the sizzle. The steak is the substance. A school may not have a successful athletic program, but may possess an intangible that is far more important. In this instance, the educational vehicle for rigorous study is housed in a warm, supportive, and caring institution. It is the people who count, not the number of buildings or the size of the football stadium. To be able to grow personally, you usually must have a personal experience.

A university that has no TAs (graduate students teaching under-graduate courses) and has an average class size of 25 with a maximum of 35 is priceless. Less is more in terms of the quality of education. Professors will know your name and will be available for discussions with you. Of course, this type of school often has a higher tuition.

If you accept the premise that college is *not* a four-year expendi-ture but a 45-year investment in the future, then it makes sense to commit to the best school that fits your budget. If you amortize the cost differential over those years (45), the savings in a less expensive, larger school (for example, one with 20,000 undergraduates) is mini-mal to almost nonexistent. It is our mantra that personal education, all things considered, generates the best return of any investment in your lifetime. This chapter will guide you in making decisions that focus on the "steak" rather than the "sizzle."

Table 5.1 : University A	
School	Departments
School of Business	Accounting, Finance, Management, Marketing
School of Science	Biology, Chemistry, Physics, Psychology
School of Liberal Arts	English, History, Philosophy, Political Science, Sociology
School of Engineering	Chemical, Civil, Electrical, Mechanical

UNIVERSITIES VERSUS COLLEGES

Although there are some colleges that are like the typical university, and some universities that are more like a large college; in general, a university is a collection of colleges or schools. Table 5.1 shows the typical structure of a university.

In making your selection, think of the college (or school) you are planning to attend, and the department within that school, rather than focusing on the university as a whole. Much of your education and career preparation takes place within your major field of study. This means that it is important to see whether that department offers a suitable "home base" for you during your college days.

COLLEGE DEMANDS AND EXPECTATIONS

A key to selecting a college is determining whether it is a good match for you. A college that evokes an enthusiastic response to challenges in some students produces disappointment and frustration in others; one that fosters intellectual and personal growth in some stifles others. The term "environmental press" has been used to indicate the kinds of expectations students encounter in their everyday experience with faculty and fellow students. In one college, you may find lively discussions, in and out of class, and considerable interaction among faculty and students. In another, the main focus may be on partying; classes are something that faculty and students tolerate. We recall an instance of a student who selected a college only to find that, unlike her, most of her fellow students there had little interest in learning. She was dissatisfied there and soon transferred to a more suitable college. Another student found herself in a place where the students split into two groups: conservative Christians with strong traditional beliefs, and the "party crowd" that rebelled against conformity. Since she had more liberal beliefs and was a serious student, not a reveler, she felt unhappy and out of place. She transferred to another college where the atmosphere was more consistent with her values, and she loved it.

COMPETITIVE OR COOPERATIVE ATMOSPHERE

Most differences are less extreme than this. There are, for example, colleges where the atmosphere is heavily competitive and a good bit

THE UNIVERSITY'S MISSION STATEMENT

Read the mission statement of each institution you are considering. It tells you much about what that college values.

Just as you peel the layers of skin from an onion to arrive at the core, you should carefully examine the colleges you are considering. Look beneath the surface characteristics and get at their core values.

of independence is expected, and others in which there is considerable support from faculty, fellow students, and other institutional resources. Some students thrive in one, some in the other.

UNDERGRADUATE TEACHING QUALITY

Two of the most important ingredients to look for are: 1) that the university has a high quality of undergraduate teaching; and 2) that class size is limited, ideally, to no more than 30 students. Educational excellence is, almost always, very personal. We believe that there is an inverse relationship between a student's ability to learn and grow and the class size. Of course, small class size does not come cheaply.

The mission to teach young people during the transitional years from teenagers to responsible, self-reliant, young adults is, on reflection, both an awesome challenge and an exhilarating experience. If the professor is willing to make the commitment, teaching can be a most demanding, emotionally draining, yet rewarding career. The professor's success in any one semester can bear fruit for decades. The legacy of good teaching is almost limitless.

The professor/student partnership must be a shared responsibility. This relationship, to be effective and long lasting, must be built upon a foundation of mutual respect, trust, and passion for learning. Of the three, respect is the most important.

The classroom experience is minimized if either you or the professor does not play an active role. The tenet of mutual respect is fundamental to the concept of recognizing the dignity of every individual.

If the professor seeks to have students grow in self-esteem, personal pride, and enhanced understanding, students must be challenged through academic rigor. Learning is arduous and the professor must motivate each learner to extend beyond his or her comfort zone. We remember the teachers who cared enough to demand excellence. With the passage of time, we are grateful for that experience.

THE COLLEGE CURRICULUM

Let's assume that you have chosen the College of Business Administration with a major in finance. Keep in mind that though many universities offer a finance major, no two will have the same curriculum. Therefore, the search for the right school for you begins with a comprehensive reading of each school's curriculum. This menu of courses may be found on the school's Web site or in its catalog, which will be mailed to you by the admissions office upon request. Table 5.2 illustrates a sample curriculum for a university student majoring in finance in the university's business school. It should be noted, however, that each major field of study has its own requirements. Every college or university has a set number of credit hours that fulfills an undergraduate degree; the combination of courses in your major, core curriculum courses, and electives comprises the credit hours that build up to this degree.

EDUCATIONAL AND SOCIAL CONSIDERATIONS

In addition to selecting a college and a major, you have a number of other decisions to make. The students you associate with, for example, will have a huge impact on your college experience.

Colleges often have honors programs, interdisciplinary programs, and special residence facilities for special interest groups. Since these options influence the kind of students you interact with, you should be sure to look into such programs when considering your choices.

Besides academics, one of the most important considerations in deciding whether a college is right for you is the campus lifestyle. It is the setting where you will be living and socializing while you are learning, so it is something you will want to look into carefully.

TABLE 5.2 : College Curriculum for a Finance Major

The University Core Curriculum = 17 courses

- 2 writing (two semesters, or a full academic year)
- 1 communication (public speaking)
- 1 mathematics
- 1 computer science
- 1 natural science
- 3 social science (economics, political science, psychology, or sociology—pick any three)
- 2 religion
- 2 philosophy
- 1 literature
- 1 history
- 1 fine arts or foreign language
- 1 additional course in either literature, history, fine arts, or foreign language

The above are the core curriculum courses required of every student in the university. The classes on the right are additional classes that are required of every student in the School of Business who is majoring in finance.

Religious Affiliation

Many private colleges are affiliated with religious denominations. These colleges usually emphasize the development of moral values in their mission, but they vary widely in the programs they use to accomplish this. Most religious colleges welcome students of all faiths, backgrounds, and philosophies; some of these colleges require religion courses, and a few require attendance at religious services. If the mission statement of the college is consistent with your values, you will want to consider such a college. Just be sure to look into the everyday life of students to see if the atmosphere is compatible with your goals and interests.

The School of Business Core = 12 courses

- 2 accounting
- 2 finance
- 1 marketing
- 1 law
- 1 international business
- 1 business perspectives
- 1 organization behavior
- 1 management information systems
- 1 business problem solving
- 1 strategy formulation (working in teams)

Finance Major Requirements = 4 courses

- 4 finance (in addition to the 2 from the Business Core)

Free Electives = 7 courses

TOTAL = 40 COURSES

Commuter or Resident Student?

The general opinion in the academic community is that you get more out of college when you reside there. You are more fully involved in activities and exposed to more facets of college life. There are, however, some exceptions. During this period when young men and women are struggling with issues related to becoming independent adults, some students do better living at home and making a more gradual transition to independent young adulthood. Another exception is if your college of choice is near your hometown and you are looking for ways to cut college costs; for some students it is a workable solution to commute from home if that means cutting out dorm fees. If these situations are similar to your circumstances and the right college is within commuting distance, you may want to consider this option.

If you commute, you miss out on life in the residence halls; it is important, however, that you do not allow yourself to miss out on campus life. Don't simply arrive for your first class and leave immediately after your last one. Seek out activities that appeal to you, and get involved. Join a club for commuter students. Arrange to eat dinner on campus and spend an evening there from time to time. Be available for some weekend activities. By making the extra effort to participate in extracurricular activities, you will ensure that you are getting the most out of college and that you are involved in campus life.

Urban or Rural Setting?

Is it better to attend a college located in or near a city, or one in the country? Before answering this question, it is worthwhile considering the advantages and disadvantages of each. Many students end up working in an urban area when they graduate. Getting to know city life while you are still in college can facilitate this transition. Also, by choosing a college in a city you will have more opportunities for part-time jobs, internships, and community service activities. On the other hand, the wide variety of available activities in a city may be a distraction from course work, so you need to discipline yourself and manage time wisely.

Social and Cultural Activities

Colleges situated in a metropolitan area provide opportunities for far more off-campus social and cultural activities. Not only are there museums, theatres, orchestras, professional sports, restaurants, coffee houses, and clubs, but there are other colleges nearby, whose resources you can utilize. Some cities have a reputation as a good "college town" because of the variety of activities and the interaction and collaboration of students from several colleges. Many colleges take advantage of resources available in the community by integrating them into their course work.

Some colleges, whether urban or rural, provide plenty of opportunities for social and cultural activities; in other places, you are more on your own. Usually, there are a wide variety of activities and organizations available on campus from which to choose. Students working on the college newspaper might have interests that differ from those in theatre groups; different fraternities and sororities often have varied goals; clubs aimed at science majors will have different activities than clubs aimed at sociology majors. As a college student you might choose activities that are closely linked to your major or that are focused on your most passionate interests; you could also decide to participate in a broad variety of activities, trying activities you haven't tried before. You will get out of your college experience what you put into it, so make sure that the colleges you are considering will provide you with plenty of opportunities to explore and develop your interests.

Co-operative Study and Internship Opportunities

Some colleges offer opportunities for students to do an internship or to participate in a co-operative study program. In the internship, you are a trainee working under a supervisor in a professional setting. In a co-operative program, you work in a full-time job as a paid employee for one or more terms. You make up class time in the summers or during a fifth year.

Perhaps the greatest change in undergraduate studies in the last 25 years has been the expansion of co-operative education, including internships, into most academic programs. Prior to this period, co-ops existed but were restricted to a few disciplines such as accounting and engineering.

The differences between the co-op and the internship are primarily money and full ime versus part-time work. Students enrolled in a co-op work full-time for a semester with a major firm and are often paid well. An internship usually consists of a part-time position while still attending class and without remuneration.

The rationale for co-ops and internships is to enhance your perspective. You learn experientially and, it is hoped, return to campus with a newly discovered motivation to achieve. In most programs, the co-op fulfills the requirements of one course as a free elective.

In some cases, you can attend summer school to complete courses missed while working and still be able to graduate in four years. In other settings, you may need to attend college for a fifth year.

Often, the co-op is a catalyst in changing your focus. You may have an epiphany wherein you realize that a career in your chosen field would not be fulfilling. This is the primary purpose of the co-op: to get hands-on experience that gives you a perspective beyond what is available from a textbook or in a classroom.

The co-op program can also play a significant role in preparing you for entry into the profession you have chosen. Think of the co-op as a barometer that provides insight into the ultimate question: What do I do with my life?

Historically, the co-op has been beneficial for both employers and students. Student feedback supports the co-op as a substantive and enriching experience and for its positive impact on the undergraduates' résumés. Employers continually support the concept that co-op–experienced graduates have a more sophisticated work ethic and are savvier about navigating the workplace than their peers who did not pursue the work option.

Graduates who have served a co-op or internship not only have a broad general education with an emphasis on the studies in their major, but also practical work experience that appeals to prospective employers.

Looking into a college's co-op programs and internships is an integral part of finding the right college. Some places have a wide variety of programs that provide relevant experience; others have few choices or offer mainly routine positions where there is little chance for development. Then, too, you will find that some colleges are located in cities with thriving industries in areas related to your career plans, whereas others lack such resources.

Study Abroad Opportunities

The second most significant change in the last 25 years in undergraduate studies is the study-abroad concept. Students are provided the option of fulfilling curricular requirements by taking some courses in a foreign country. Most colleges offer this opportunity at about the same cost as a semester on campus. You spend one or more semesters in another country taking courses, usually taught in English, for one semester or one academic year (two semesters).

The main advantage of the study-abroad program is cultural: You learn much more than the academic components of the courses in which you are enrolled. An appreciation and understanding of the culture of the host country is significant, and possibly, life altering. If English is not the first language of the host country, you have an opportunity to acquire a second language. Additionally, living in another country can generate many intangibles. A new understanding and appreciation for a way of life that had been foreign to you is a most desirable byproduct. With the growing interest in international understanding—both as part of the student's general educational development and as a way of broadening career opportunities—study abroad is an invaluable experience.

This program is not to be confused with "Travel Study Courses," wherein the class visits a country for a week or two with one or more professors. For example, a class in addictions counseling that has been studying the topic during the spring term could include in the syllabus a visit to a few countries during the spring break. They can observe how various countries approach the prevention and treatment of alcohol addiction and other drug abuse.

Since study abroad can enhance your educational experience, it is worth looking into the availability of such programs. Some colleges have connections with international universities or are part of a consortium of colleges, whereas others administer their own program. In many cases, study abroad costs no more than a comparable time of study at the student's university.

COMMUNITY COLLEGES AND DISTANCE LEARNING

Attending a community college for the first two years is another option to consider when you are looking at schools. If there is a high-quality community college nearby and it has a program consistent with your career plans, you can usually save money with this choice. While there are advantages to attending the same college for four years it is important to consider the pros and cons of residential college versus community college before making your decision.

If you choose to attend a community college for the first two years, plan your program so that you are able to make a seamless transition to a four-year college without having to repeat courses or attend for an additional year. To do this you will need to research the credit transfer agreement between the community college you select and the four-year college to which you want to transfer. For more information on community colleges, check out the listing for The American Association of Community Colleges in the Appendix.

Distance learning can make it possible to take college courses, and even to complete your college degree, using the Internet. When weighing the option of distance learning it is important to remember that while it may be a more convenient and less expensive way of taking classes, it will not provide the same learning experience as attending classes with other students. Still, it is useful under certain circumstances. For example, taking summer courses in this way can reduce your schedule and your cost during the academic year. It is also worth considering if regular college attendance is not feasible.

CRIME ON CAMPUS

When looking at colleges, parents (more so than their children) worry about campus safety. Parents tend to be concerned that there is more crime in urban areas, and that therefore urban colleges are more dangerous. There is a kernel of truth in this, but the perception is not necessarily the reality. The danger of being a victim of violent crime is often greatly exaggerated by some families, who then rule out a college in an urban setting on this basis. In actuality the greatest risk of harm to college students is from automobile accidents. If safety is an overriding concern in choosing a college, the amount of driving needed to get around and the road and weather conditions under which the bulk of this driving will occur should be a more important consideration.

In terms of violent crime on campus, it should be noted that the perpetrators of campus crimes are often fellow college students. When looking at schools, parents and prospective students should be aware that colleges are required to keep a public record of incidents of crimes that take place on and near the campus. Keeping these records and making them part of the public record is mandated by a federal law called the Clery Act. The Clery Act is named after Jeanne Ann Clery, a freshman who was raped and murdered in her Lehigh University dorm room by a fellow student in 1986.

Unfortunately, colleges are often inconsistent in how accurately they report information about crime on campus. Some, for instance, classify burglaries (which must be reported) as thefts (which need not be reported), which gives that campus artificially low crime statistics. In fact, a Justice Department survey in 2005 found so many irregularities in reporting that only one-third of colleges were fully consistent with the law.

NARROWING YOUR CHOICE

There are a number of sources to help you narrow your choice. Most are useful, but none are definitive. *US News & World Report, Money Magazine,* and several other magazines provide ratings of colleges that you should review to gain information about possible selections. Criteria for the best colleges in the 2007 *US News & World Report* rankings included racial and ethnic diversity, average freshman retention rate, average class size, faculty resources, and SAT/ACT percentiles.

There are also standard reference works that usually give general information, and publications by college students that are more impressionistic and often based on a very limited sample of students. You should also check Web sites of prospective colleges and read their brochures and other literature.

Keep in mind while sorting through these materials that you are looking for colleges that will be a good match for you: not *the best college,* but *the best college for you.* A successful college graduate that we know was pleased when he was accepted to Cornell, which he knew was an excellent college based on its rankings and on the research he had done. It turned out, however, that he felt lost by Cornell's large size and his new surroundings. He later transferred to a smaller college where he felt more comfortable and where he did well.

At this stage of the process you are not making your selection, but narrowing the search by eliminating colleges that are not compatible with your plans and selecting those that you want to consider.

THE COLLEGE VISIT

One of the best ways to narrow the number of colleges on your list is to visit as many as you can.

Importance of the Visit

Visiting a college before making a final decision is a must. Yet some students choose a college based on information provided on the Web or in printed material. They often discover that the reality is far different from the advertising or from the college's reputation among fellow high school students.

A telling illustration of the importance of the visit is the case of the young man who was determined not to attend the college his father had gone to. The more his father encouraged him in that direction the more determined he grew not to go to that college. Finally, to placate his parents, he agreed to make a campus visit on his own. After meeting with faculty and students, he returned home to announce his decision: "I can stop looking now. That is the college for me!"

Another student had been telling her parents for several years that the selection of a college was easy. She had read a great deal about a particular college and knew it had a fine reputation. That was where she was going. When she finally visited the place, she had a complete change of heart. "I'm certainly *not* going there!" she told them.

Preparing for the Visit

To get the most out of your visit, be prepared. Read the material in advance and know what you want to look for, what questions you want to ask, and to whom you need to speak. We have seen families show up at a college without an appointment after driving a long distance, only to find that the people who have the answers to their questions are not available. You may want to include time for just wandering around the campus during your visit, but you don't want this to be the *only* thing you do!

The Superficial and the Substantive

At one time, college students led a rather spartan existence. Today, many students are looking for a relatively luxurious lifestyle during their college years.

June Kronholz writes in *The Wall Street Journal* that some universities are getting "building fever." That is, big-ticket amenities are added to college campuses and students often foot the bill.

Colleges are adding amenities to rival those of a five-star hotel. Majestic structures and creature comforts, including dining facilities, fitness centers, theaters, and student union buildings, make an excellent first impression on visitors and often have an undue influence on the selection process.

The same can be said of the millions of dollars spent on football and basketball as recruiting tools. Many people tend to judge the worth of the college by the size of its football stadium and basketball arena and by the caliber of its athletic teams.

It is much more important to find out about the quality of the teaching. A college's reputation for teaching excellence may take a decade of sustained effort and passionate commitment to achieve. Unequivocally, great professors are the essence of a great college. Nothing is more important! How faculty and staff relate to students and how students relate to one another is the key. Is there a personal, caring environment with a commitment to students? It is ironic that prospective students and their families are often unduly impressed by an attractive campus or a successful athletic program, and miss out on looking into the essential academic features that produce a great college.

Organizing Your Visit

Plan to spend enough time on and around the campus. Arrange to stay overnight in a residence hall. Schedule times to meet with appropriate administrators and times to sit in on classes. Most important, be sure to talk to the students. Have your questions ready before your visit, and know whether an administrator, a faculty member, or a group of students would have the most accurate answer to each question. Here are some examples of questions you should consider:

- Does it typically take four or five years to earn a bachelor's degree at this school?

- Would you come to this school if you had the chance to redo the decision?

- Is it true that some professors grade differently than others in the same department?

- What is the average class size?

- Do you have TAs (teaching assistants, typically graduate students) grading your essay exams?

- In which majors are students receiving job offers as they complete their degrees?

- What percentage of the pre-med students are accepted into medical school?

- What percentages of students are accepted into law school or graduate school?

- Do you have access to your professor in his or her office? Or, must you see the graduate assistant?

- If the university provides financial grants, are they for the first year only, or are they renewable for each year?

- Is dormitory living provided for all four years, or just the first year or two?

- Are the dormitory rooms doubles, triples, or greater?

- Can one live in the dormitory in a single room?

- Why are some students anxious to move to private off-campus housing?

Admissions, Financial Aid, Student Life, and other administrative divisions of the university can provide answers to many factual questions. However, the single most effective tool to dig for answers about the atmosphere of the college, both in and out of class, is the student cafeteria at dinnertime. The students are relaxed and convivial. It is your opportunity to ask questions of a group of people who are not in a hurry and who enjoy the opportunity to be the "experts." Observe the students while they are eating. Do they seem like a friendly and congenial group? Place some trust in your intuitive abilities in judging whether you would fit in. After watching for a while, take the initiative and ask some of the questions listed above. Listen closely to the responses. Talk to several different groups. Be friendly and assertive. Most students are glad to speak openly with visitors.

WHEN THE RIGHT COLLEGE TURNS OUT TO BE WRONG

Despite all of your effort to find the place that is best for you, it is possible to end up in a college that you really do not like. We know of several students who selected a place that seemed to be a fine choice at the time, but for whom it just did not work out.

This is not a time to berate yourself, or believe you have ruined your chances for success. This is where the work you have done in planning for college can pay off. Reconsider your second and third choice (and maybe others). You now know more about what you are looking for. Transfer! Often students who hate their first choice love their second.

One word of caution: Don't judge whether you have made the wrong choice by the first week or so. There is often a period of adjustment when students are confused and uncertain. Give it a reasonable amount of time; if the dissatisfaction with the college persists, however, don't hesitate to make the move to another place.

Chapter 6

How to Get Accepted and More

Success is getting what you want. Happiness is accepting what you get.

—*Dale Carnegie*

I wouldn't want to belong to any organization that would accept someone like me.

—*Groucho Marx*

A few years back, it was discovered that, for one question, the answer key to the PSAT was incorrect. This test, taken in the junior year of high school, determines which students are awarded merit scholarships. The error was revealed when a student who was confident he had all of the answers right on the quantitative section of the test was told that he had one wrong. (The question asked the number of sides in a figure that resulted from joining two pyramids with a different number of sides). His answer proved to be right and the key answer wrong.

This change in one question resulted in hundreds of additional students being awarded scholarships. Although in theory small differences in credentials are insignificant, this illustrates that in actual practice small differences often determine who gets accepted and who is awarded a scholarship.

In another instance, a student who had been accepted to the college of his choice was reluctant to retake the test when his school was taking it as a group. However, he made a much higher score the second time and, as a result, obtained a substantial grant from the college. It should be noted that if you take an admissions test twice, both scores will be reported. However, admissions administrators usually give more weight to the higher score since it is a better reflection of your potential.

Most students, even those with average abilities, are able to get accepted at some college in some program. To improve your chances of getting into one of the better colleges, in one of the better programs, or to obtain a scholarship or other forms of financial aid, it helps to have strong credentials. It also helps to plan the application process so that your strengths are highlighted.

THE APPLICATION PROCESS

This chapter explains what goes into the application process and how to prepare for each part. It also gives practical tips to highlight your past accomplishments and your potential.

High School Record

Since the best indicator of future achievement is past achievement, the best measure of your likely success in college is how well you have performed in high school. This record of your high school grades is called your transcript. The first thing college admissions officers consider in evaluating an applicant is the quality of the high school attended, the type of courses completed, and the grades earned. So, if you have attended an academically strong high school and have obtained high grades in demanding courses, you are off to a great start. If you have not done as well, but have some time left, now is when you should start to improve. It may be too late for some colleges and some types of financial aid, but there are some ways in which a marked improvement, even late in the game, can broaden your options. Such improvement demonstrates that you are capable of doing the academic work, and it gives an indication that you are willing to do so.

Background Check

Increasingly, colleges are asking applicants and guidance counselors to provide information about criminal or disciplinary incidents in the student's background. Cases of driving under the influence, fighting, cheating, theft, and so on, are setting off warning flags in college admissions offices. Admissions officers might ask themselves if they want to accept a student with a poor disciplinary background or if it is just asking for trouble to admit that student. On the other hand, if the incident was minor and the student has since stayed out of trouble, it might demonstrate to the admissions office that the student has learned from his or her mistake.

THE APPLICATION

Currently, over 300 colleges require a form known as The Common Application. It is an admission application that you need complete only once, and you can send it to as many of the participating colleges as you wish. This saves the time of filling out separate applications to each institution. It is available online and in print. Its use is limited to colleges that use a holistic selection process, including recommendations and at least one essay examination question.

This application form includes information about past disciplinary information. How colleges assess this application and how they check on its accuracy varies, but all agree that lying about past infractions is a sure basis for rejection. Some states are also running background checks on all new college students in that state as a way of screening for serious criminal behavior.

Making a Favorable Impression

In completing the application and personal statement, be sure that it is neat, well written, and free of careless mistakes. If you are applying online, print out a copy and have it checked before you send it. Save a copy of everything you send for your own reference and in case something is lost. Make a note of all deadlines for each college and submit all material ahead of time.

Tailoring Your Application to the College

In addition to providing information about yourself, your application package should also indicate in your personal statement the reasons why you have selected this particular college. Demonstrate that you know its mission and traditions, and state why you believe it is a good match for you.

A generic statement that does not mention the name of the college, or an application package sent to USC that states why you are interested in UCLA (yes, this does happen) obviously detracts from your application.

PERSONAL STATEMENT

Much of the information about your achievement in high school is easily available from your transcript. It is a good idea, however, to highlight your successes in a statement that you submit with the application. For example, if you did well in particularly demanding courses, or if you improved significantly after a slow start in your first year, be sure to point these things out. If you have overcome handicaps, or succeeded academically despite other time-consuming responsibilities, this is worth mentioning (although it is best done without excessive elaboration). Keep in mind that it is unlikely that you can explain away a poor record by putting some kind of positive spin on it in your statement, like the student who wrote, "The fact that I failed English three times before finally passing it is a good indication of the kind of persistence I have."

You may want to point out why you have taken advanced languages or modern art rather than more science, or why you have taken certain advanced placement courses. Other activities that you have been involved in are also worth including. If you were active in athletics, or chess, or debating, you should indicate how these experiences have helped you develop and prepare for the future rather than merely listing them. However, keep in mind that dabbling in a large number of activities is often seen as less desirable than a more serious commitment to fewer activities.

If you have been involved in volunteer work, study abroad, or research, or if you have held part-time or summer jobs, you should likewise do more than simply list them. Briefly describe how you have benefited from each experience, and discuss what this tells about your abilities, interests, and maturation level.

Be forewarned: attempts to be clever or "creative" in your personal statement are more likely to create a negative impression unless they are done well. This includes personal statements that contain inappropriate self-disclosure and for ideas that may seem bizarre to the admissions committee (avoid mentioning the fortune teller who predicted that you will become successful and famous or the aliens from outer space who speak to you!). It is best to have your personal statement checked by a knowledgeable adult who can serve as a mentor during the application process.

LETTERS OF RECOMMENDATION

When you are competing for college acceptance or financial aid, your recommendations can tip the scales for or against you. The most important decision is who to select as your references. Usually, letters from physicians, pastors, local politicians, relatives, and employers carry little weight. It is assumed that they know little about your academic ability. It is also a mistake to select teachers or other references merely because they are friendly and approachable. A teacher with whom you have done excellent work is in a far better position to help you to stand out with a recommendation letter. Furthermore, if you have done a significant project, whether in school or outside of it, the person who supervised this work would be a logical choice to ask for a recommendation.

In addition to considering how well your references know your abilities, it may help to choose someone whose opinion carries weight with the college. If a teacher is an alumnus of the college or if you know another influential alumnus who can cite evidence of your abilities (perhaps a business or civic leader), you should consider asking him or her. Be careful with this, however. If it is interpreted by the admissions committee as an attempt to use improper influence, it could backfire and hurt your chances. Once you have selected your references, help them to do the best job for you. Here are some suggestions:

1. Ask them if they would be willing to write a letter of recommendation for a given purpose. Explain what you want to accomplish and find out whether they are willing to support you. If it is evident that they have reservations about it, thank them and find someone else.

2. Provide your references with a written statement of your background, accomplishments, and goals. This will make it easier for them to write a strong recommendation and to do it in a timely manner. And don't forget to provide a stamped and addressed envelope.

3. Allow enough time for your references to write the letter well before the deadline. You will want your letter to be sent at least a week before the deadline, and you should allow a minimum of two additional weeks for the letter to be written.

4. Read the instructions carefully, and be sure to follow them. Is there a form for your reference to use? If so, are you to complete part of it? (Often students will request a letter of recommendation and supply the letter writer with a form on which they have neglected to complete a section that is supposed to be done by the student). Have you specified the correct and complete address to which letters of recommendation should be sent? (They often end up in different offices or even different colleges).

5. You are normally asked whether you wish to waive the right to see the letter. This is a matter of judgment, but it is generally agreed that when the applicant waives this right the letters carry more weight. It shows that you are confident that the person you have asked to write a recommendation will write a positive one.

6. Be sure to thank those who have written letters for you and to let them know the outcome. Not only is this the right thing to do, but it also helps if you have occasion to request their help again.

THE SELECTION INTERVIEW

In some cases when the selection process is highly competitive, candidates with excellent credentials are called in for an interview before a final decision is made. You may be asked for an interview by one or more faculty or staff, or you may be invited to meet with an alumna or alumnus who lives near your hometown. Evaluating candidates in this way is admittedly subjective, but it helps to know what characteristics typically enhance or detract from the impression a candidate makes.

Preparation has a major impact on how a candidate is evaluated. Supplying the interviewer or the committee with background information about you well in advance of the session is essential. It also helps if you bring extra copies for every member of the committee in case they have been misplaced by the interviewers. In addition to providing information about yourself, you should study the university to which you are applying and the nature of any grant for which you are being considered. Know the mission and history of the university, the purpose of the grant, and be able to describe how your background and goals are consistent with these.

First impressions make a difference. Clothes that are right for a party or are customary for lounging are inappropriate for an interview. Your dress, posture, speech, and ways of interacting with interviewers create an impression that influences how subsequent material is judged. A student who arrives late, is dressed casually, looks down at the floor and mutters comments will be judged negatively compared with one who shows up ahead of time, is conservatively dressed, stands up straight, looks directly at the interviewer and speaks clearly and carefully.

There are two extremes in your interactions with interviewers that can give them a negative impression of you and damage your candidacy. One extreme is being so passive that it is difficult for an interviewer to draw information out of you. The other extreme is being too assertive or abrasive, and dominating the conversation without listening to the interviewers. These extremes are typically exhibited by students trying to mask their nervousness. Fortunately, most interviewers expect you to be nervous and accept it. Do not focus so much on hiding your anxiety that you miss out on the points that you want to make.

TAKING ADMISSIONS TESTS

In addition to the above indicators of your aptitude, most colleges give some weight to your performance on standardized admission tests in making admissions decisions. In this section, we intend to demystify these tests and help you learn how they are used and how to do well in them.

The main tests used in evaluating college applicants are the Preliminary Scholastic Aptitude Test (PSAT), the Scholastic Aptitude Test (SAT), and the American College Test (ACT). The PSAT, normally taken in the junior year of high school, is also used as the National Merit Scholarship Qualifying Test. (See Chapter 3 for more information.)

The PSAT and SAT, or College Board, consists of three parts:

- Critical reading (formerly verbal)
- Math problem-solving skills
- Writing skills

The SAT also provides subject matter tests in the following areas:

- English literature
- U.S. history
- World history
- Mathematics
- Biology
- Chemistry
- Physics
- Languages

The ACT (see ACTTest.org) includes tests of the following areas:

- English (usage, mechanics, rhetorical skills)
- Reading comprehension

- Mathematics pre-algebra, algebra, geometry)

- Writing (optional)

Based on the results of your ACT test and a questionnaire covering your interests, high school courses, and career plans, an ACT Assessment Student Report is developed. Reports are sent to you, your school, and any college or scholarship source that you request.

Being at Your Best

Although many young people believe that they are not affected by lack of sleep, the evidence shows otherwise. Most teens require seven to nine hours of sleep for optimal functioning. Lack of sleep before a test day causes difficulty in concentration and increases the likelihood of making careless mistakes. To be at your best during the test, you should go to bed a little early the night before (and even the night before that), get up in time to eat a healthy breakfast, and arrive at the testing site without rushing and with time to spare.

If you are regularly taking medication, check with your doctor as to whether you should make any change in dosage on the day before or the day of the test. Otherwise, avoid alcohol, sleeping pills, or other medication. Drugs are more likely to interfere with test performance than improve it. In one case, a student showed up on the day of a test obviously agitated. With his body trembling and his voice shaky, he admitted that he had taken some Benzedrine in the hope of being alert, but that he was unable to concentrate or sit still, and couldn't take the test.

Test-taking Strategy

Some students are "test wise," meaning that they are able to demonstrate their aptitude and achievement very well in taking multiple-choice tests. Other students, who are just as bright as the test wise, have difficulty with the multiple-choice format. There are students who might fail a multiple-choice test despite the fact that they can answer questions from the same material with ease when they were asked in an interview.

What follows are some tips to improve your performance on various types of tests.

Mistakes to Avoid

The term "multiple guess" has been used so often that some students approach the test as if it were a guessing game when, in fact, each question actually has a best answer. A careful review of the question and a comparison of the choices can pay dividends if you are unsure of an answer.

A related mistake involves a kind of superstitious behavior in seeking clues to the answer in things that are irrelevant. Going by the length of the answer, believing that "C" is the most common correct choice, or assuming that since the answer to the last question was "B," it couldn't be the answer to the next question are examples of the kind of self-defeating approach that some students adopt.

You may be uncertain what to do when you are unsure of the best answer. Generally, you should not waste time mulling over such a question, but should make an intelligent guess and move on. Usually you can eliminate some choices and improve the odds of getting it right. The main exception to this recommendation is in subject matter tests. Here, it is better to skip difficult questions initially and allow time to return to them at the end. Often, as you answer items you know, it will help you recall answers to material you had forgotten.

Concentration

Another kind of self-defeating behavior is mindlessness or not disciplining yourself to concentrate on the test questions. It is probably impossible to concentrate for every second during a test, but you can learn to develop sufficient discipline so your mind is not constantly wandering throughout the test. You can improve your concentration by taking practice tests and noting how long you are able to concentrate without a noticeable distraction. As you continue to practice, you will gradually increase the time between distractions so that it is no longer a handicap.

Using Time Wisely

If you are nearing the end of the allotted time and still have questions unanswered, should you just fill in answers to have something down? This depends on the test. For the PSAT and SAT the answer is "no," since points are subtracted for wrong answers; for the ACT, where you are graded by the number right, the answer is "Yes." In general, it helps to know the scoring method ahead of time to guide you in your test-taking strategy.

At the start of the test period, note the number of questions and the time allowed. Use your test booklet for scratch work. Mark questions you have omitted so you can go back to them if you have time. As you are taking the test, keep track of your progress to see if you are moving at the right pace. If you have time left when you have finished the test, use it to check for omissions or obvious mistakes rather than agonizing over some item in which you are unsure of the answer. By learning to manage your time well during tests you will avoid both dawdling and putting yourself under excessive time pressure.

MATHEMATICS

When preparing for a test, it is most important to know what subjects will be covered. Otherwise, you may spend time studying trigonometry or calculus when the test questions cover only algebra and basic geometry. In taking practice tests, a key point is not to look at the answers first. After you have answered all of the questions, check which ones you have wrong and note the kind of mistakes that you have made. This will broaden your skills and prepare you for whatever the SAT or ACT throws your way.

When practicing for tests, it is best to solve a group of problems that require you to use different formulas or procedures rather than spending time working on a series of problems that require the same approach. This will show a pattern of the kinds of mistakes you are likely to make and help guide your studying to improve your weaker areas. As you learn to solve new problems, be sure to compare the new process with methods you had learned earlier to solve different problems.

When doing mathematical problems, be sure that your answers make sense. You can make a rough estimate of the answer by working with rounded numbers. For example the answer to the problem (3,729 X 624)/97 should be roughly equal to (4,000 X 600)/100 (24,000); if you came up with 313,927, you know that you must have made a mistake.

The mathematics content of the SAT includes advanced topics. The following math concepts are covered on the test (this list can be found on the College Board's Web site):

Numbers and Operations

- Arithmetic word problems (including percents, ratios, and proportions)
- Properties of integers (even, odd, and prime numbers; divisibility; etc.)
- Rational numbers
- Logical reasoning
- Sets (union, intersection, elements)
- Counting techniques
- Sequences and series (including exponential growth)
- Elementary number theory

Algebra and Functions

- Substitution and simplifying algebraic expressions
- Properties of exponents
- Algebraic word problems
- Solutions of linear equations and inequalities
- Systems of equations and inequalities
- Quadratic equations
- Rational and radical equations
- Equations of lines

- Absolute value

- Direct and inverse variation

- Concepts of algebraic functions

- Newly defined symbols based on commonly used operations

Geometry and Measurement

- Area and perimeter of polygons

- Area and circumference of circles

- Volume of boxes, cubes, and cylinders

- Pythagorean theorem and special properties of isosceles, equilateral, and right triangles

- Properties of parallel and perpendicular lines

- Coordinate geometry

- Geometric visualization

- Slope

- Similarity

- Transformations

Data Analysis, Statistics, and Probability

- Data interpretation

- Statistics (mean, median, and mode)

- Probability

WRITING

The best way to prepare for an essay test is to regularly practice writing essays in which you give yourself a 25-minute time limit and have a teacher or writing tutor review the essays and give you suggestions for improvement. You should follow a series of steps to facilitate writing essays for tests, such as:

1. Select and clarify your topic. Even when a topic is assigned, there is usually considerable leeway as to how it can be approached. Read the directions carefully. Be sure you are answering the questions that are asked, not something only distantly related to them.

2. Decide the approach you are going to use. You may consider a cultural, a historical, or perhaps a personal perspective. You may also select a major topic with several subtopics. Jot down aspects of the topic that come to mind. One topic leads to another, so you should soon find that you have plenty of material to draw from.

3. Organize the material you have, grouping similar items, deciding which topics are major issues and which are subordinate or illustrative. Ask yourself whether you agree or disagree with the author's position and what examples might support your position. This should enable you to draft an outline of your paper.

4. Follow your outline and write your first draft. Use a separate paragraph for each major subtopic, starting with an introductory paragraph that gives an overview of your essay and ending with a concluding paragraph that summarizes what you have written. Each paragraph should begin with a topic sentence that provides a transition from the previous one to the new subtopic.

5. Revise once or more as needed until you have a satisfactory essay. This includes the way you have organized your thoughts and expressed them in a manner that demonstrates your fluency with language.

In taking the essay test, be sure that you are not too brief. This is a mistake many students make. Don't cut a good example short to rush on to another point. It is better to have a comprehensive paper with good ideas that would benefit from revisions than to spend so much time thinking about the best way to express each point that you get very little down on paper.

CRITICAL READING

In the critical reading portion of admissions tests, the usual format consists of a passage of reading material followed by one or more multiple choice questions on its content. It is not necessary to memorize the passage but only to be able to answer the questions about it. Usually it is better to first skim the passage to get the general idea, next read the first question and then find the answer in the passage (if you do not already know it). Another strategy, particularly if it is a lengthy essay, is to start with the questions before looking for the answer in the essay. Keep in mind that questions on critical reading are not limited to factual information, but may include intent or attitude of the author and editorial devices being used.

APPLIED KNOWLEDGE

The study skills and habits you employ in preparation for college application tests will serve you well in your college studies. Vocabulary building and active reading skills, while useful for the writing and critical reading portions of application tests, will be useful to you in just about any course of academic study.

Vocabulary Building

Although the PSAT and SAT no longer include separate tests of vocabulary, building your vocabulary is still one of the most effective ways to improve your score on the essay and the critical reading portions of admission tests (PSAT, SAT, ACT) and to help you prepare for college. Vocabulary building improves your language comprehension and your facility in expression of your ideas. To a large extent, vocabulary building occurs through reading, listening, and studying course material, because this is how you encounter new words. It also helps to get in the habit of jotting down (or underlining) words when you are uncertain of their meaning and then looking them up in your dictionary. You should keep your eyes peeled and your ears pricked for new words, to help build and maintain a strong and useful vocabulary.

Rather than trying to learn large numbers of esoteric terms, it is better to concentrate on words with which you are familiar, but whose meaning is vague to you. You may have come across the expression "arms akimbo" on several occasions, but have only a rough idea of its meaning. Check it out! It is also a good idea to study words that are commonly confused, such as *effect* and *affect* or *perspective* and *prospective*. Learn to distinguish them with confidence. This helps critical reading and writing ability.

Frequent brief review sessions also work wonders with vocabulary. Learning and reviewing a few terms several times a day is a useful approach. Vocabulary cards, which are handy to carry in a pocket or purse, are a convenient way of doing this. Regularly using the dictionary is also a good habit to develop.

Active Reading

An active program of reading a wide variety of both nonfiction and fiction is another great aid in intellectual development and personal maturity. It also helps to prepare you for college and for the tests that check your aptitude for college.

One of the main characteristics that differentiate the highly successful from the less successful is that the former are active rather than passive readers. Active readers jump right into the material to see what they can get out of it, rather than simply drifting without focus. Active readers typically move faster, speeding up on passages that are clear or repetitive and slowing down on important points or on sections that are difficult. When they underline, highlight, or take notes, active readers do so only for points they want to review. (Some students go overboard and highlight every sentence in a chapter; this is simply a waste of time.) The active reader also asks and answers questions about the content of the reading. "What did the author say was the most important cause of the Civil War?" "Which states joined the Confederacy?" "What was the short-term impact of the Emancipation Proclamation?"

It is also important to schedule time to review what you have read. Much of what you learn in the initial study session is quickly forgotten, but it can be quickly relearned. It is inefficient to spend the time it takes for initial learning and not take the briefer time to review and improve your retention and comprehension of the material. For example, if you studied a chapter of history for two hours, and by the next day, have retained only half of its content, a 15- to 20-minute review will enable you to relearn most of it. Some subjects—foreign languages, mathematics, and certain aspects of science—especially require frequent review for adequate retention.

SUMMARY

Keep in mind throughout the application process that you are looking for the college that is the best match for you. The Deans of Admissions are trying to determine if you are a good match for their college. You are working toward the same goal, although from different perspectives. You should be able to help one another arrive at a mutually satisfactory decision.

Chapter 7

Academic Success and Its Value

My son didn't go to college to fool around; he went there to learn.

—*Rose Alito, mother of supreme-court justice Samuel Alito*

Success is one-tenth inspiration and nine-tenths perspiration.

—*Thomas Edison*

Academic achievement is not simply a matter of obtaining grades or honors; it is a reflection of competence. Students who use their opportunities wisely become more proficient in their profession and in their general ability to function well and achieve a sense of satisfaction. High school and college should be times for developing in many ways, but particularly in the depth and breadth of your knowledge. Unfortunately, some students have accepted the stereotype in which the high-achieving student is depicted as a nerd who can't find the way to the restroom. Although there are a few students who are excessively bookish pseudo-intellectuals, typical high-achieving students are more successful and feel more fulfilled than average students.

PREPARING FOR ACADEMIC SUCCESS

Some high schools are called college preparatory or "prep" schools. They are private schools with rigorous academic programs whose mission is to prepare students for college. Most public high schools are multipurpose institutions, intended both for those who are preparing for higher education and for those who are going directly into the work world. If you are considering college, you can help yourself get ready for that transition by taking a strong academic program and forming effective work habits while you are in high school. Advanced placement

(AP) courses are highly desirable in this way. They provide a taste of what college courses will be like, as they cover more complex material and require more self-sufficiency. In addition, you can obtain college credit for them. Nationwide, about 14 percent of high school seniors satisfactorily completed at least one AP course in 2006. The number of students taking such courses has been growing, as has the number taking college courses while still in high school.

High school is also a time to develop effective work habits. Unfortunately, some bright students manage to complete high school, and even obtain high grades, despite sloppy work habits. This chapter includes tips on developing good work habits that help ease the transition to college (and help develop good life skills to boot).

MAKING THE TRANSITION TO COLLEGE

For some students, the transition from high school to college is relatively smooth; for others, there is a need to reexamine their approach to academic work and to upgrade their self-discipline and study skills. This is due to the fact that college is a different environment than high school. In most cases, high school tends to be a regimented institution in which the faculty and administrators micromanage the students' entire day. Student behavior is closely monitored and controlled by numerous rules and regulations designed to maintain discipline and order. College, on the other hand, lacks this structured environment. Homework, for example, might be assigned, but possibly not collected or checked. Class attendance is rarely monitored, allowing students to cut class with no immediate repercussions. Ironically, some students are unable to function effectively in the university arena because they find it difficult to adjust to the responsibilities that come with having so much freedom.

RESPONSIBILITIES IN COLLEGE

Class times at college vary. A schedule of four or five courses that meet for 50 minutes each three times a week means that you spend only 12 to 16 hours each week in class. If, however, you rely on the benchmark that suggests you spend two to three hours outside of

WHAT TO EXPECT AS A FIRST-YEAR STUDENT

As a first-year student you will:

- Face ethical issues that need to be confronted and addressed. There may be problems relating to your roommate, dating difficulties, harassment, and plagiarism, to name a few. Do you have the maturity to seek help from your faculty advisor or the campus counseling center?

- Have to develop an infrastructure within the campus community. Can you balance all the requirements of daily living, including basic tasks such as doing the laundry, cleaning your room, and eating a nutritious diet?

- Be accountable for what you do and have to accept responsibility for your actions.

- Have to complete the assigned readings with systematic discipline. Much of the professor's classroom agenda assumes that the outside assignments are completed and understood.

- Have professors who may never check your work, nor seek you out for incomplete work. You must contact the professor about such issues during his or her office hours. These times are usually posted and listed on the course syllabus.

class for each hour in class, the sum is striking. The suggested outside class work ranges from 24 to 39 hours per week!

These calculations explain why so many first-year students do so poorly academically. Simply, those who fail or fall short of expectations, in most every case, have not made the necessary outside-the-classroom commitment. (Some don't even make the inside-the-classroom commitment!) Maturity, focus, discipline, and systematic study habits are the ingredients required to achieve academic success. There are no shortcuts in the long run.

Since college students have considerable freedom, some of them misuse it. Doing little or no work, the immature or undisciplined student coasts through the first few months of college, missing classes frequently, doing little homework, and putting off assignments. All too late, the student realizes that a semester's worth of work cannot be crammed into the last few weeks.

It has been our experience that women seem to mature earlier than men, and hence, tend to have more patience and persistence in the first year of college. Although some men excel in their freshman year, others do not excel until later in their college career. For the latter, there is a risk that they will respond to initial academic frustrations or setbacks by quitting. They may not necessarily drop out of school, but will instead abandon systematic and rigorous study habits and resign themselves to mediocre performance and thus not get the most out of their education.

When you begin college, your parents will not be there to cover your back. Metaphorically speaking, you are free to steer the college ship in any direction. No one else is establishing the parameters for when you go to bed, when you go to class, when you study, or when you work on course assignments. You are the one with unlimited freedom and total accountability. Freedom, for the irresponsible and immature young person, is often detrimental to his or her studies.

Since you have to manage your own time, certain skills, if not already honed, must be developed quickly. Are you capable of managing your time and setting priorities? You must be able to say no to some activities and not waver from that decision. No one is going to demand that you get out of bed in the morning. If you have an 8:00 A.M. class, you must resist the late night socials, whether they be in your dorm or at a local bar or pizza parlor. You must also decide what, if any, extracurricular activities you will participate in. You must find a balance between your academic and your social lives and adhere strictly to this agenda.

In balancing your social life with your academic life, it is important to note that, in college courses, testing is usually infrequent and often covers large amounts of material. Makeup tests or extra credit work are seldom an option. Furthermore, several exams are often scheduled in the same week. That means that it is important to have your class notes organized in a way that provides the most complete feedback in the shortest format possible to make the best use of your out-of-classroom study commitment. Life, including academic life, isn't always fair. Grades on tests and course papers are the significant components of the course grade. Class participation is usually not a part of your grade. In fact, in many universities, participation is discouraged, especially in a class of 600 students. Rather, you are expected to withhold your questions until you have the weekly class with the TA. The particular style is a function of class size. In other universities, however, the class size may be 20 to 25 students. In this setting, class participation is encouraged and even expected.

Please remember, it is normal to be frightened, homesick, and nagged with doubt during the first three or four weeks. These emotions are, in fact, a sign of intelligence. Fear of the unknown generates this human response. But after the first month or so, these insecurities are generally a distant memory.

THE VALUE AND LIMITATION OF GRADES

It is not uncommon to find college freshmen who are upset at receiving a grade of "C" or lower. "I don't understand it," they complain, "I am an 'A' student." Such students need to modify their self-concept or their work habits, or both. Not everyone can or should expect to get As—certainly not in every subject. There are too many other things to accomplish in college to become obsessed with grades. Even students who know the subject best do not always get the highest grades. We recall a time when most of a class was in the library studying furiously for a physical chemistry test scheduled for the next day. One student, however, was browsing through a book on paleontology. When he was asked why he wasn't cramming for the exam, he said that he knew what he wanted to learn about physical chemistry, and he wasn't concerned about his grade on the test. He had studied regularly during the term, understood the material, and had no need to cram for the final examination. He went on to become a successful physicist.

That having been said, it is still desirable to have a strong academic record. Admission to graduate or professional school is influenced considerably by grades, and companies recruiting for some of the better jobs often consider only students in the top portion of their class.

Yet, grades are not an end in themselves. They are intended to be a reflection of how well you have learned and how capable you are of learning new material. They show your capacity for abstract thinking, for completing complex tasks well, and for expressing your ideas in a clear and convincing style. As you develop these abilities, you may find a joy and satisfaction in the learning process itself, so you approach course material and other new challenges with enthusiasm and confidence. When this occurs, you have become a real student: an active, rather than a passive learner. This cannot be measured with a grade.

SELF-DISCIPLINE AND LEARNING

One of the main ways to facilitate this transition from passive to active learner, and an invaluable resource for your future success, is to develop good work habits. Set aside regular times for study and

DEALING WITH THE FEAR OF FAILURE

The greatest teacher you will ever have is failure. It provides more of an opportunity to learn than success, yet far too many students hesitate to take on responsibility or try a new activity because of a fear of failure. It is a common reason for procrastination and a source of self-imposed stress. It is important to remember that mistakes and misunderstandings are natural with any new endeavor. The usual way we improve is by trying an activity, finding out what we are doing that is right or wrong, and learning from this. The only real failure is in not trying: or in not seeking and using feedback about our performance.

stick to them. Have a place where you are free of distractions, or where they are at a minimum. Turn off television and cell phones and put a "DO NOT DISTURB" sign on the door, or use the library or another quiet area.

The difference between academic success and failure is not intelligence or SAT scores, and certainly, it is not luck. Rather, it is daily study in a disciplined and systematic manner. Following this practice guarantees (yes, guarantees) success in school. The development of this kind of self-discipline also guarantees (well, almost) success in your future career. With few exceptions, most students who have gone on to make outstanding contributions in their professions are those who have learned to take advantage of the time and resources available while they were in college.

BASIC PRINCIPLES OF SUCCESS IN COLLEGE

Now that the basics of preparation for college have been covered, this section will focus on your use of these points both inside and outside the classroom. This should not only prepare you to do well in college but should help you achieve success in the real world.

In the Classroom

It is not uncommon for academic departments, such as Accounting, Nursing, Education, Engineering, and Psychology, to be subjected to criticism by some of the people who work in the profession. These practitioners frequently assert that the undergraduate course content is too theoretical or irrelevant in the workplace. This may be true, but what the professional misses is that learning the theories of a discipline may allow a student to apply those theories to other situations and adapt to systems in the real world.

If college professors were to teach a specific modus operandi, the graduate would only be able to function in that one system. By receiving a solid theoretical foundation, a student entering the workforce is able to quickly learn the specific applications used by an employer. The goal of college is to teach students how to learn. If students are grounded in the conceptual understanding of the model and have developed the learning-to-learn concept, they will always have the skills necessary to adapt to change. This is one of the major purposes of a college education.

College is not designed primarily to prepare you for a particular occupation. Rather, by teaching you how to read with comprehension, to write with clarity, to analyze problems, and to express ideas effectively, the college experience confers to you the ability to embark on fulfilling careers of your choice. Let's examine each of these academic goals.

Reading with Comprehension

You learn to read with comprehension by reading complex material that is not readily understandable. In many courses, you study such thinkers as Plato, Aristotle, and Socrates. Although the material may at first appear to be "Greek" to you, it will gradually assume meaning after you learn (with the professor's help) to break down and understand difficult material. Like any skill, this takes effort and discipline.

The most important part of most college courses is not the content but the process. Class material may be forgotten; learning how to learn will stay with you.

Writing with Clarity

Although most high school students probably consider science or mathematics the most important subjects to master, it is our opinion that the most important subject in high school and college is English. Every person, regardless of the area of expertise, from accounting to zoology, must be able to express himself or herself in written form. This includes your ability to organize your ideas in a meaningful way and to compose sentences that are effective in communicating your points to your audience. To be able to do this clearly and convincingly is a major mark of an educated person. Few of us can do this naturally. To develop this skill takes a lot of practice, coupled with temporary failure. In our illustrative curriculum (Table 5.2 in

Chapter 5), the student will write a minimum of 17 short papers in the freshman year.

If you are fortunate enough to have a professor who meticulously corrects your essays, you will grow exponentially as a writer. Please remember, it can be a painful process. Try not to personalize the instructor's notations on your essays. Without an objective critique of your work, there would be little improvement in your writing skills. Again, temporary failure is the greatest teacher you will ever have.

Analyzing Problems

Many students excelled in their early educational years by memorizing instead of comprehending. At some point in your college career, you will find that this no longer works. In a philosophy class, for example, there is no single correct answer. It is not the solution, but the methodology used to arrive at an answer that matters. The journey toward discovery is more important than the destination.

In many other disciplines, the answer to a problem is not the primary objective. Accounting, for example, is an art wherein the answer to a question is secondary to the process of solving the problem. You usually learn more in the search for a solution than in its discovery. In some classes, you will be given a homework assignment requiring an hour's worth of effort. If you can complete the task in less time, fine, but it is important not to quit after five minutes if you are stymied. Even if the answer remains elusive after an hour of work, the struggle to find the solution will boost your analytical and critical thinking capabilities and make the professor's solution in the next meeting far more meaningful.

You must think analytically in philosophy and accounting, and in life. This skill is required at every level in the post-college years. A key part of analytical thinking is figuring out what questions need to be asked. In *The World Is Flat*, Thomas L. Friedman tells of Nobel Prize winner Isidor I. Rabi being asked how he became a scientist. He replied that every day after school his mother would ask, not what he had learned in school that day, but, "Did you ask a good question today?" "Asking good questions," he said, "made me become a scientist."

Speaking Effectively

The ability to express your ideas clearly and convincingly is one of the most difficult and most important skills to master. Some of the brightest people have difficulty in this area. Many universities require a communication course in the first year in which students in a small class take turns speaking before the group. These short speeches are often videotaped by the professor, while the rest of the class completes a questionnaire evaluating the performance in a variety of categories. Invariably, the first speech is a disaster, which students realize after viewing the tape. They are surprised to learn how often they repeat expressions such as "you know," "like," and "uhh." Although you may be discouraged initially by the ineptness of your presentation, over the course of the semester your confidence and skill will improve. Obviously, some people will have more of a natural talent in this area than others, but everyone will improve in a substantial way.

STUDY SKILLS AND THE LEARNING PROCESS

Dr. Rooney remembers an instance of a student whom he taught. This was a first year student and he had trouble completing his work and the quality of his work was consistently below the standards set for the course. Three years later, Dr. Rooney had him in a class again, this time as a senior. The student's performance had changed dramatically, so that he was one of the better students in class. The difference? He had worked past his earlier academic struggles and learned the skills needed to feed the learning process. The skills needed to be successful.

Initial Learning

In learning new material, start with an overview and then move to the specifics. In studying a chapter in a textbook, for example, first skim the chapter to get a general idea of what it is about. Then read the chapter, moving quickly over easy or familiar material and slowing down when you encounter new or more complex concepts. Underline, highlight, or make notes of important points and terminology. Review these points until you know them well, being sure that you also know the main themes in the chapter and how the points are related to it and to one another.

If you have set aside a long time period for study (for example, five hours in a given day), it is better to divide it into two or three parts, with a break in between for some variety and to keep your mind fresh. Hint: this is a good time to get in a little physical exercise.

Review and Relearning

Research shows that much of what we initially learn is very quickly forgotten. This is truer for rote learning than for material that we have been able to understand, integrate, and relate to what we already know.

Fortunately, we can relearn material we have forgotten rather quickly. This means that it is more efficient to spend time reviewing material we have studied until we know it well than it is to constantly move on to new material that we quickly forget. Such review can be accomplished in brief periods such as when moving between classes, waiting in line, during commercial breaks on TV, or riding as a passenger in a car. If you have a part-time job, you will probably have short breaks that you can use in this way.

Certain subjects and certain topics in other subjects require frequent review to resist forgetting. Mathematical equations, foreign language, and terminology in every subject are examples of material that needs to be memorized and reviewed. Using index cards as a study aid is a good way to keep your review materials handy at any time. It is also helpful to spend some study time at night, especially before you go to sleep. Less forgetting occurs during sleep than at any other time. Evidence shows that this is because sleep optimizes the consolidation of information that has been recently acquired and helps it "stick" in your mind.

Memorizing Versus Understanding

In many subjects, an understanding of the material and an ability to relate concepts to one another, to organize, integrate, and criticize are more important than rote memory. Here you read not merely to acquire new facts, but to gain new perspectives. Throughout your reading it is best to pause frequently to reflect on what you have read, to ask yourself questions, and to consider the implications that flow from the content. It helps to practice making up questions that test your knowledge of the topic, and see if you can answer them. As a general rule, you should spend more time answering questions about the material than in the initial reading.

BECOMING AN ACTIVE LEARNER

Someone has defined a classroom lecture as "a situation in which material passes from the notes of the instructor to the notes of the student without going through the mind of either." Clearly, there is little teaching or learning going on in such a situation. Your study time outside of class can be shorter and more productive if you use your time in class wisely. Some students sit passively daydreaming, or are easily distracted, or write notes from the lecture routinely without any thought. Some students even fall asleep in class. How, then, can you best use your class time to become an active learner?

Learn to Accommodate Different Teaching Styles

It is commonly known that different students respond better to certain teaching styles. They do well with some teachers and poorly with others. In an ideal situation, all of your teachers would be outstanding at their craft and would teach in a way that appeals to every student. In actuality, there are usually some faculty members who have wide appeal with students, a few (hopefully only a few) who are generally considered poor teachers, and many who some students like and learn from readily, while other students have difficulty. A key point in becoming a strong student is to learn how to learn in different situations and with different teaching approaches.

Just as you vary your study approach with different subjects, you can learn to do it with different instructors. If the lectures are difficult to grasp, for example, try reading the material on the topic ahead of time. Then, if there is a point you don't understand in the reading, be ready to ask a question to have it clarified. If class participation is important, plan ahead so that you can make a positive contribution during class discussions. If assignments are not clear, ask the instructor, not another student. In general, be an active learner. Get to know other students in the class who like the course and are doing well. You might soon find their interest rubbing off on you.

Note Taking

It pays to have a systematic way of taking notes during class and of retaining and organizing them for review. Note taking should help you stay focused during class, listen for important information, and provide an aid for effective review. Usually, a list of main topics and subtopics with a few important points will suffice. It is counterproductive to try to transcribe the professor's every word. Trying to copy everything gets you focused on the individual words and sentences rather than on the meaning of the material.

A good way to cement your learning is to review and reorganize your notes after class when the material is still fresh in your mind. This is especially useful if your notes have been hastily scribbled and you have trouble reading them after a few days.

WORKING WITH YOUR PROFESSORS

A college student told Dr. Rooney that he had read a piece on how to make a good impression on the instructor. He said it recommended sitting near the front and toward the center of the class, nodding in agreement with points the instructor makes, smiling broadly if he says something humorous, jotting down notes as he makes important points, asking an occasional question, and when the class period ends, continuing to check your notebook for a minute or so before leaving.

He seemed a bit puzzled, "Would this really work?" he asked. What could any instructor say but, "You're darn right it would."

Dr. Rooney once taught a student who was also a star athlete. This student always arrived well ahead of time, sat in the front, with text and notebook open. His whole posture and attitude sent the message that he was ready to go all out. His performance in the classroom was like that in the basketball arena. He pushed himself to learn as much as he could and kept pushing until the bell.

In contrast, another student was going away for the weekend and planned to miss an early morning class on Monday. On Friday, she asked the instructor, "Are you going to cover anything important on Monday?" She failed to recognize the sarcasm when the instructor replied, "No, we're just going to fool around like we usually do." She said, "Oh good!"

It is important to realize that faculty members are a resource to help you become an educated person. Utilize the variety of approaches and talents they provide to facilitate your learning. Faculty members are not your adversaries—they are your advocates. Your success is their success. In a sense, pursuing a college education is like climbing a mountain. Some of the faculty will be pulling and others pushing you up the incline, all the while assuring your ascent with safety ropes. This is especially true in a teaching-oriented, rather than a research-focused, university. In the former, where small class sizes are the norm, the relationship between professor and student is often a more personal one. Even in the larger universities, most professors maintain office hours to give students an opportunity to speak with them. During these times the instructor has made a commitment to be in the office and available for students to visit and discuss any of their concerns.

Unfortunately, many freshmen do not take advantage of this invitation to speak with their professors on a one-to-one basis. It is usually the more successful students who visit during office hours. They do so to clarify lecture material, obtain input on research papers (such as suggestions on topics or sources), or to seek advice on future course selections.

Think of the student/professor relationship as a joint adventure. The two of you are going to row a boat out beyond the horizon to explore lands that you have never seen before. If your oar is not in the water, however, the boat will move around and around in circles, but will not make any progress, as the instructor rows furiously but you do nothing.

Forging the student/professor relationship is not a question of seeking favors from the professor. Rather, it is one of gaining favor. How do you do this?

- Go to class! Get in the habit of attending class and getting the most out of each one.

- Be on time. Better yet, arrive ahead of time and get to know some of your fellow students.

- If you miss a class, get the notes from one of your classmates.

- Visit the professor during his or her office hours with whatever questions you have about the class. If you never do this, you are missing an opportunity to get the most out of the course.

- Get assignments in on time.

- Don't expect an extended deadline. Usually, late assignments are hurriedly done and of poorer quality than those that are effectively planned and completed on time.

- Never discuss a grade when you are angry. Seek an explanation in a courteous and professional manner. Never use the word *unfair* when discussing the grade with the professor.

- Sit in the front half of the class. Always bring a notebook and the textbook, if appropriate. The message is direct. You are prepared and interested.

OTHER LEARNING RESOURCES

There are a number of other resources available to assist your intellectual development besides the faculty. Knowing these and taking advantage of them can be a definite aid in getting more out of your college education.

NO EXCUSES

Professors don't want to hear statements such as the following:

- "I didn't have time to do that."
- "Another student told me we didn't have to do that."
- "I didn't understand what you wanted."
- "You didn't cover that question in class."
- "I didn't know that was plagiarism."
- "I think the grade you gave me is unfair."
- "I was up all night doing this...."
- "I got the wrong advice."
- "Do we have to buy the textbook?"
- "This assignment is too hard."
- "Is this going to be on the exam?"
- "Did we do anything important in class today?"
- "I couldn't study because I...:
    - broke up with my girlfriend (boyfriend)."
    - lost my book (my notes)."
    - had a major assignment (exam) in another class."
    - had an important game (practice, meeting, job, party)."

A final one is, "I've been trying to get in touch with you." Which upon further checking usually means: "I've been thinking about getting in touch with you, but never got around to it."

Fellow Students

None are more influential than the fellow students with whom you interact. A few friends with whom you form a regular study group or with whom you can exchange ideas about course material and other topics can be a great resource for your academic growth. On the other hand, associating mainly with students who are indifferent or negligent can detract from your progress.

Librarians

Another important resource for learning is the library, and, in particular, the reference librarians. They can assist you in learning how to utilize the library resources, including electronic resources, effectively in writing reports and working on other projects.

WRITING PAPERS

Writing assignments are an essential part of college learning in just about every subject. The amount of writing you do and the quality expected is another adjustment you need to make in moving from high school to college. As with studying and organizing your time, you need to develop strategies to undertake this part of the college experience successfully.

Value

Writing research papers, journals, and laboratory reports is a valuable part of your academic development. Most professional and business careers require the ability to locate and organize appropriate information and to write a clear and effective report on it.

STEPS IN WRITING A PAPER

Some students have learned the basics of writing a paper in high school and arrive at college prepared to write papers; unfortunately, other students have not mastered this skill and find themselves struggling to make the transition to college coursework.

The most common problem students have with writing papers is procrastination. A paper that is due in two months is often put off until a few days before the deadline, leading to a last minute scramble for information, and an all-night session of writing. It is much better to plan a schedule in which you have target dates for the most important steps:

1. Select the general topic.

2. Narrow or delimit the topic.

3. Develop a list of sources to consult.

4. Read and evaluate material and take notes.

5. Organize the material and write a first draft.

6. Revise until you have your final paper.

If you follow these six steps, the outcome is generally a paper that you can feel good about and that increases your confidence in your abilities. This approach enables you to break the complex project into a series of simpler steps, which can then be tackled individually. This keeps a topic from seeming overwhelming. It is important to consult the instructor (or teaching assistant) after each step to see if you are on the right track and to obtain suggestions for improvement. Learning to use this approach while you are in college is an enormous help in completing projects you will encounter in your career after you graduate.

Evaluating Sources

In researching material for a paper, you will find inconsistencies and contradictions. Some of this is a reflection of the current state of knowledge in the field, but some is because a good bit of misinformation and biased material finds its way into print and, to an even greater extent, onto the Internet. A valuable ability to develop is the capacity to judge how reliable a resource may be.

Articles that appear in a professional journal typically have high standards for accuracy and are a more valid source than an opinion someone has posted on a Web page. In general, avoid using references that are out of date. You should look for references that reflect what is current knowledge in a given topic. How recent this is varies with the topic (and some older references may be useful for giving a historical perspective or for other purposes). Usually, original material from professional journals is superior to popular journals and to secondary sources, such as textbooks.

Avoiding Plagiarism

In writing papers, be certain not only to avoid blatant plagiarism, but also its more subtle forms. Most students know full well that it is wrong to copy from another student or from a book or article. Many students are not aware, however, of the many forms plagiarism can take and are shocked at being called out on it. They may also be unaware of the possible consequences of being guilty of plagiarism. Depending on the instructor, the college, and the nature of the plagiarism, punishment up to suspension or dismissal from college is possible. Some plagiarism is readily detected by the instructor just by reading the report. Other cases can be identified through the use of computer programs designed for that purpose.

The key points to avoiding unintentional plagiarism are not only to cite all references that you use, but to clarify when you are using the words of an author (by using quotation marks or block quotes) and when you are using the ideas of an author but stating them in your own words (by citing the author). Keep in mind that taking large segments of the author's work and simply changing a few words or sentences is not acceptable.

EMOTIONAL MATURITY AND ACADEMIC PERFORMANCE

Your emotional maturity plays a significant role in how you perform academically. As a first-year student, you may want to ask yourself the following questions

1. Do I have the maturity to appreciate the opportunity that a college education provides?

2. Do I have the patience to acquire wisdom?

3. Do I expect to find happiness in college?

When considering the first question, first-year students would be wise to understand that knowledge is the power to control the rest of their lives. Education is the catalyst for economic opportunity. The mature student recognizes this and takes advantage of what is truly a once-in-a-lifetime opportunity: the chance to grow intellectually, socially, and emotionally while still unburdened by most familial or employment obligations.

When considering the second question, it is important to realize that wisdom differs from knowledge that comes from books. You must acquire it from life—from both success and failure. In many cultures, the elders are considered the wisest because of their experience, including their experience with failure. Wisdom comes over time. Do you have the patience it takes to acquire wisdom?

When considering the third question, you need to examine not just your expectations of college but also your self-esteem. Not unlike the principles established in a book by Don Miguel Ruiz entitled *The Four Agreements*, it is important that you embrace a personal philosophy of daily living that lessens self-denigration. What matters most is how you feel about yourself! If you feel good, you are blessed. If you find yourself frequently thinking negative thoughts about yourself and your competence, think again. Focus on positive and realistic goals that you can achieve and experience the feeling of success.

If there were one gift we could bestow on every student in the first week of college, it would be a strong self-image. Unfortunately, only you can provide yourself with this priceless gem. That is why it is called self-esteem. A positive mindset is "money in the bank" for success in college and in life. Here are a few hints for developing self-esteem

- Avoid criticizing or judging others.

- Never accept someone else's criticism as accurate. Weigh it before you decide whether to use it.

- Never assume anything. Do not hesitate to ask questions. Whether it be with a professor or a classmate, be assertive (not aggressive) in the pursuit of clarity.

- Always do your best. Sound simple? It isn't. Like any skill, it takes practice. There will be times when you will be stressed or fatigued and will underperform. Occasional lapses are to be expected, but there is no excuse for chronic underperformance.

- Give to others and you will be on a road that leads to happiness. Have you ever analyzed careers that generate happiness? Invariably there is a common theme: helping others!

- Enjoy your work. Many students select majors that they believe will lead to jobs that will generate a large financial return on investment. What they fail to appreciate is that psychic income (loving what you do for a living) is of more value than monetary rewards. If you like English literature, history, or political science, don't be afraid to major in it. You may be surprised to discover that you can earn a living and still enjoy your work.

SUMMARY

Although this chapter has focused on academic and intellectual development, this is only one part of your college experience. You don't just send your mind to college. You are there as a total person with physical, social, emotional, and spiritual interests; you want to develop as a total person. In organizing your time, plan for physical exercise (preferably including a team sport), social activities (including at least one organization where you can develop leadership experience), and other kinds of recreation and relaxation. This kind of balance not only helps you develop as a total person, but also permits you to approach your studies with more enthusiasm and effectiveness. Getting enough sleep is highly desirable, not only for your health, but for your ability to function effectively. Seek out social affairs where there is little or no drinking (at least by you) rather than all-night parties that leave you with a hangover or worse for the next day or two.

It is good to develop friendships, particularly with students who have similar values. It is also worth broadening your horizons by making friends with people of different backgrounds and from all walks of life. At the same time, it is desirable to have your own inner compass, so you don't simply go along with others, but do what you believe is best.

Chapter 8

Personal and Emotional Maturity: the Social Side of College

Friendship is the hardest thing in the world to explain. It's not something you learn in school. But if you haven't learned the meaning of friendship, you really haven't learned anything.

—Muhammad Ali

No one can make you feel inferior without your consent.

—Eleanor Roosevelt

The first year of college may be the most profound year in your life in terms of change. You may experience periods of low self-esteem, high anxiety, homesickness, and myriad related symptoms. It's okay. Within one month, many of these feelings will have faded. Do not give up prematurely.

PERSONAL DEVELOPMENT

As you mature, you should not only learn to choose your activities wisely, but should move toward greater independence from peer pressure and a greater reliance on your own values. College is a time in your personal journey through life where change is very possible. It is your choice. Is a more mature lifestyle better than the one you have lived to this point? All that is required is the courage to try, determination to stay the course, and a willingness to start again when you fail.

We recall a senior mentioning that one of the main changes he noticed about himself was in self-determination. "When I was a freshman," he said, "I would go along with whatever the crowd was doing; now I decide for myself and don't hesitate to say 'No' and set my own priorities."

Certainly, college is a time for trying new experiences and for learning from your mistakes, but you can also use the experience of others and your own ability to anticipate the consequences of your actions to avoid making too many mistakes or any critical ones.

As you steer your ship through the sea of life, you alone are at the helm. You must take responsibility for the ship's destination. Live life on your terms, not someone else's! No doubt, there are alumni who look back on college days wishing they had taken things less seriously. There are probably just as many who wish they had been more serious about their work.

Intellectual development is an essential part of personal development. It helps give you a sense of perspective, a feeling of competence, an ability to evaluate new ideas, and confidence in expressing your own point of view. If you develop social skills while you are in college, but miss out on improving your mental prowess, you are missing a significant part of personal development.

There is a saying in finance: "No risk, no growth." The student who has a balanced college experience will be the more successful graduate. As in any investment, without risk there is little or no return. In a stock portfolio, it is recommended that you have a variety of investments, including some that are a bit risky but may surprise you with a big payoff. In a similar way, you are investing in college to learn and grow as a person, but learning is not confined to what is required by the faculty. Plunge into the pool of available activities. Take a course in fine arts, write for the student newspaper, or become a DJ at the campus radio station. Take your work seriously, but don't take yourself too seriously. Try new things. You are 18 years old. In all likelihood, you are filled with uncertainties. As someone has said, "Work like you don't need the money, love like you've never been hurt, and dance like nobody's watching."

Know Thyself

One of the oldest and most often quoted pieces of advice is the inscription on the Oracle of Apollo at Delphi, Greece: "Know thyself." If we might accept this as a starting point, we would modify it for the contemporary student to say, "Know yourself; accept yourself; improve yourself."

In some ways, most of us know ourselves well. We know our height and our weight, how fast we can run, and what kind of food we enjoy. In many other ways, we tend to distort or misjudge our talents, our potential, and our affect on other people. Getting to know ourselves involves getting to know other people. It also involves testing our limits, taking on challenges, stretching our minds, and seeing how we function under widely different circumstances. In getting to know yourself, however, you should avoid certain common mistakes.

All or none thinking. This is the belief that you are either great at something or a total failure: the smoothest person on the planet or a complete klutz. Like most people in the world, you are no doubt ordinary in a lot of ways. It helps to recognize this.

Using a distorted mirror. Some people look at themselves and focus on the flaws. It's valuable to be able to see ourselves as we are, warts and all, but some see only the warts and miss the total picture.

Accepting feelings as truth. If you feel unattractive, then you believe you must be unattractive. Learn not to be overly influenced by your emotional state in making judgments about yourself.

Reliance on the opinion of others. Too often, students base their self-concept on what others believe (or what they think others believe) about them. While you cannot completely ignore the views of other people, you should learn to evaluate yourself independently.

Accept Yourself

One of the wonderful things about human beings is that each is unique and complex, with unique talents and aspirations, limitations and foibles. We see this and admire it in our friends, but usually fail to respect it in ourselves. We should feel good about ourselves even though we want to improve during college and beyond. This change is seldom easy. There is a tension between the way we have been and the way we want to become, and between the world we came from and the world we are moving into. This conflict is often especially prevalent in students who are members of minority groups. If you have grown up in a minority subculture, you may have learned that the world is a hostile and dangerous place. Most students face such conflicts, but to a lesser degree than minority students who have been discriminated against. Our advice: start by accepting yourself! Learning ways in which people differ from one another contributes to everyone's education. You should feel good about yourself and your background. An important part of education is to get to know and appreciate people from different backgrounds and cultures. That is one reason why colleges look for diversity in recruiting international students, and students with varied, geographic, religious, ethnic, and socioeconomic backgrounds.

Improve Yourself

First-year students need the opportunity to grow as individuals. Sue Shellenbarger of the *Wall Street Journal* mentions several skills that students need and often lack:

1. Being assertive in pursuing what you need

2. Being considerate of sharing the dorm room

3. Being independent and self-reliant when facing challenges

4. Being attentive to your spending habits

College provides a supportive place to begin the pursuit of personal freedom. You can gradually learn confidence in speaking out in an effective way for what you truly believe, rather that being overly concerned with pleasing faculty members and fellow students. At the same time, you can learn to respect others and listen to their opinions even when you disagree. A mature person can disagree without being disagreeable.

It is imperative that the college student, especially the freshman, learns to become assertive in matters of importance. Whether it is your roommate, classmate, or professor, you should learn to initiate respectful and focused dialogue to address any problematic issue.

The growth of your self-esteem is in jeopardy if you repress your instincts to correct the unacceptable. The ability and willingness to be assertive, not aggressive, is a learned skill like any skill, failure is often more frequent in the early stages. But it becomes easier and more natural over time, as long as you don't give up. Remember, repetition is the mother of all learning.

When you have achieved that level of development, you can truly echo the words of Dr. Martin Luther King, "Free at last, thank God Almighty, free at last."

ROLE MODELS AND MENTORS

One of the most common ways we learn is by observing how others behave in various situations and modeling our behavior after them. This kind of imitation may be intentional, or it can occur without our being aware of it. The term "role model" is used for persons we admire and want to be like, at least in certain respects.

Dr. Rooney asked a class of students to name someone who served as a role model for him or her. The most common response was a parent or other family member; some chose media stars from movies and television, athletes, pop musicians, or political leaders; still others picked characters from history or fiction. Throughout your college experience, you should encounter people, real and fictional, who serve to influence and perhaps inspire you in this way.

A mentor may or may not be a role model too. He or she is someone you work with closely who knows a good bit about the system or organization within which you are working. In college, it is usually a faculty member, or one of the staff or possibly an upper-class student. It is worthwhile making the effort to find a good mentor, since you can learn so much from her or him. Faculty members typically get considerable satisfaction from the success of students for whom they have served as mentors.

FRIENDS

The friends you make in college have a major impact on your development. Not only are friends a source of fun, but you can also learn the variety of ways in which other students respond to the challenges and opportunities encountered in college. You can test your ideas against theirs. Unlike high school, college is a 24-hour-a-day experience. You eat, sleep, study, and socialize on campus. You will meet many fellow students, but choose your close friends wisely. A key characteristic in picking friends is whether you respect them and they respect you. A good friend will tell you when they think you are doing something that is out of line. Friends you make in college often become friends for the rest of your life. You may even meet your future spouse.

ROOMMATES

Your most important initial acquaintance at college is your roommate, because this is the person with whom you will be sharing living quarters. If you have a friend from high school who is attending the same college, you may assume it is an easy choice to choose him or her to be your roommate. Be careful! This is often a mistake.

Roommate trouble often stems from assuming that you will get along well; however, it is important to set ground rules for sharing the same space. Be considerate of your roommate, but be open and clear about what you expect from one another. Get agreement on specific issues that may be a source of conflict such as quiet time, visitors, privacy, and sharing or respecting one another's property. Experience shows that each roommate tends to believe he or she is taking on more than half of the responsibilities, and the other person is negligent. You shouldn't just do the jobs that you like to do or that you think are important and expect your roommate to do the rest. If he or she does the same thing, it is sure to lead to trouble.

Hint: If you like privacy, select the bed located behind the door. Since residents tend to leave their doors open in the evening (for socializing purposes), this will enable you to maintain visual (although not audio) privacy. Your roommate, on the other hand, will be seen by every person walking by. Here are a few more tips on dealing with roommates:

- Talk to your roommate about any conflicts. At times, this will be difficult. Timing is crucial. Never initiate dialogue when there is some anger in the air. At the right time, talk about the problem, not your roommate's deficiencies. Ask for his or her participation in the issue on the table. Be calm and direct. The interaction will be more successful if there is specificity about the problem. A comment like, "Being on the phone until 1:00 A.M. really bothers me," is more productive than saying, "Would you get off the stupid phone?" Discuss without assigning blame. The outcome is likely to be successful.

- Be direct with your roommate. The discussion will be beneficial to both of you if you communicate honestly. Explain exactly how you feel about his or her behavior. But, listen to the roommate's response closely, and if a valid point is made, agree unequivocally.

- Learn to compromise with your roommate. To change your roommate's habits, you must also change. To solidify the new verbal contract, it may be wise for the two of you to put it in writing. This strengthens the comprehension of what has been agreed upon.

If mediation fails, then you must consider and pursue changing rooms. Most universities have a formal procedure for implementing this process. You are required to adhere to the rules established by the Dean of Student Life. If there are no available rooms, you must cope with the status quo or move off-campus. The latter may introduce a new set of problems, including extra costs.

DORM LIFE

Life on college campuses, in its dormitories or residence halls, has been depicted in books and movies as a series of parties, pranks, and high jinks. Stories of cows and cars showing up on the top floors of the dorms, and footprints of a rhinoceros or an alien prominently displayed across the campus abound. Actually, the experiences and challenges you face in living on campus are quite different from what these stories show. Usually, dormitories are buzzing with activity.

You will have the opportunity to develop all sorts of partnerships: study partners, jogging partners, pizza pals, and other friends within the building. You will also get to know the residence advisor (RA). This is a junior or senior who serves as a mentor, concierge, and, if required, police officer. The RA, and other residence-life staff, is part of a built-in support system, especially for first-time-away-from-home students. When you have a question, or need advice, don't count on sophomores or your fellow freshmen, but check with one of the residence-life staff.

Socializing on the Internet

Students are increasingly using the resources of the Internet to reach out to new people. Facebook, MySpace, and other social networking sites continue to grow in popularity. You must keep two things in mind in using them: 1. They are not private. You may think they are only used by other students, but you should not post things there that you would not want parents, faculty, or prospective employers to see. All of them can gain access to the site to see your profile. 2. There is a safety issue, since the Internet is used by all kinds of people, including predators who use it for harassment, stalking, and other potentially harmful purposes.

It is important to do what you can to guard the privacy of anything you post on the Internet, but realize that many people will still be able to obtain access to it.

PARTIES

Some colleges have acquired a reputation as "party schools," where students spend more time and effort partying than studying. At many colleges, there are a variety of parties available, from small, friendly, relatively subdued get-togethers with little or no alcohol consumption, to all-night, drunken affairs that destroy property, injure students, and ruin reputations. Some students associate having a good time with drunkenness. A senior recounted a conversation he heard between two freshmen. One said, "Boy, did I have a time last night, I even threw up." The other responded, "You think you had a good time, I threw up three times!"

College freshman often assume that excessive drinking is a normal rite of passage for them. Yet, the evidence shows that the majority of students either decide not to drink, or drink moderately. Unfortunately, a large and well-publicized minority does drink to excess. They incur the danger of accidents, particularly automobile accidents, of arrest for driving under the influence, getting into fights, of getting involved sexually in undesirable or dangerous ways, or possibly being a victim of rape. Binge drinking, including consuming amounts of alcohol that are fatal, is all too common in some college groups. The good news is that there has been some decline in excessive drinking, as an increasing number of students recognize its dangers. The bad news—as reported in newspapers, including *The Post*, Ohio University's student newspaper—is that now the rate of alcohol and drug use is higher among teenage girls than boys. We discuss alcohol and other drugs further in the next chapter.

Gambling

Gambling among college students has become a growing concern in the past decade. As with much of the party scene on campus, some degree of gambling has become viewed as "normal." While many students are able to play a sociable game of poker or lay a wager in a sports betting pool with sensible limits for both money and time spent, others become so involved that they spend more time in playing cards and computer games than in studying. Others get such a high from gambling that it becomes an addiction, driving them into excessive debt. There are also some who believe they can make money from gambling. A few manage to do so, but most find (especially when the stakes are high) that there is always someone who is a better gambler, and some who don't hesitate to stack the deck or load the dice. When caught up in the excitement of gambling, people often forget the adage "The house always wins."

EXTRACURRICULAR ACTIVITIES

Aside from organizations associated with your major, there are a wide variety of extracurricular activities available. Students have a wide choice of out-of-class activities for enjoyment, relaxation, and social and emotional development. These include ROTC, travel groups, student newspaper, drama, music, debating, and arts, in addition to the community service activities, Greek societies, athletic groups, and organizations for students in given majors that were previously mentioned.

Some students become caught up in a whirlwind of activities with the intent of becoming a well-rounded person. Everyone cannot and should not strive to become well-rounded in this sense of the word. It is better to plunge deeply into a few activities that you value than to dip your toe into every available pond. Taking on a position of responsibility in just one organization, and learning how to handle it well, is better than being a passive member of several groups.

FRATERNITIES AND SORORITIES

First-year students are often flattered when they are invited to join one of the Greek societies during rush week when sororities and fraternities are recruiting new members. But hold on! Decide in advance whether you want to be a member of this group; don't let them decide for you. Look into fraternities or sororities ahead of time. They can be organizations that enhance your college experience; they can be sources of fun and friendship, as well as chances for service and leadership. They might, instead, be sources of immature, distracting, or even destructive behavior. Binge drinking and degrading hazing practices are still common in many Greek societies. If you are considering one of them, carefully look into its goals, its programs, and its reputation, before you join.

Presently, there is a decline in the popularity of the Greek system. It is under scrutiny as never before, especially by college administrators. The latter believe that fraternities and sororities foster anti-intellectual practices and have become a major source of campus disruption fueled by alcohol abuse. As of 2005, only about 5 percent of all college students belonged to a Greek society. Obviously, this percentage varies from campus to campus, something you can look into when evaluating colleges.

ATHLETICS

If you become a member of a college varsity team, particularly in a major sport in a division IA college, you will have to devote a considerable amount of time to practicing, conditioning, and traveling. The value of this experience need not be elaborated on here. Suffice to say, such participation requires discipline, teamwork, persistence, and competitiveness. It may also give you the opportunity to get to know a wide circle of people, including some in positions of considerable influence. Many people in high positions in business, government, and other fields are passionate about athletics; thus, participation in sports can provide an introduction to them through this common ground.

Usually, colleges have programs to assist athletes with academic work, including individual tutoring and group work to help them balance their athletic goals with their academic ones. Many athletes take summer courses or extend their programs to five years in order to reduce the course load during the academic year. Before making a commitment to one or more sports, however, you should know what is involved. A number of talented athletes decide to limit their activity to one sport or even not to participate in varsity sports at all. Others decide to attend a college where the commitment to athletics is less intense.

Dr. Reardon played varsity baseball in college. The heavy schedule of games in the spring term, the time taken to travel, and the number of absences from class (excused, but missed just the same) resulted in midterm grades that had been a solid "A," sliding to a "B." Fortunately, the difference did not turn out to be sufficiently serious to prevent him from being awarded an assistantship to graduate school, but it might have. And it was a source of considerable concern at the time. Looking back, was it worth it to devote so much time to baseball? Probably not!

On the other hand (and there usually is another perspective), Dr. Rooney ran on the track team in high school, but decided he did not have time to participate in college. Does he regret that he missed a worthwhile experience? Sure!

In any case, there are a large number of athletic teams, from varsity sports to intramural, club, or informal groups, available for young women and men in college today. There are also fitness centers, swimming pools, and other facilities for aerobic workouts. Some kind of regular physical activity is desirable for everyone, not only during college, but also throughout life.

WORK EXPERIENCE

One of the questions you have to decide is whether to obtain a part-time or summer job. For some of you the answer is clear, you must work to earn part of your college expenses. For others, college expenses are paid, but you have other needs for income.

It is usually better to take out low-interest loans for college expenses and have enough time for studies and related activities than to be so pressed for time because of working too much. It is also crucial to thoroughly (and honestly) evaluate other needs. Rather than work long hours to pay for an expensive car or an elaborate vacation, you would usually be better off to reduce this expense and be able to cut down on hours of work. Work should not interfere with more valuable activities of college life.

If you decide to get a job, don't focus exclusively on the salary. The kind of experience you get from the job, the likelihood of having time for study, and the kind of people you work with are examples of other considerations.

SERVICE LEARNING

Increasingly, college students are getting involved in community service by tutoring children, assisting the elderly, working with the poor and disabled, and cleaning up sections of the community. Service groups are using vacation time to work where there is need, whether in Appalachia, the Gulf Coast, or Mexico. In any month on any campus, students are sponsoring 24-hour volleyball marathons or similar events for some worthy cause. More and more majors have a service component linked with them. Many colleges require community service as part of the curriculum, or have community service departments that serve as resources to help you get involved. There are also many service-oriented organizations that you can seek out while in college, such as Habitat for Humanity.

Perhaps the case can be made for the importance of this aspect of a student's development by a quote from President Abraham Lincoln: "When I do good, I feel good. When I do bad, I feel bad."

MORAL DEVELOPMENT

Part of the development that takes place in college involves a maturation of your values. It would be a wasted opportunity to develop intellectually, socially, and emotionally, but to retain the moral outlook of a child or adolescent or to blindly follow the values you grew up with without reexamining them. Developing values is part of a liberal arts education. Courses in literature, history, philosophy, religion, and the social and behavioral sciences are among the resources that contribute to this. Religious services and discussion groups are often available. Most of all, learning to treat others with respect, take on responsibilities, set priorities, and make some kind of contribution to society are marks of a mature person.

Just as plants need water, sunshine, and good soil to flourish, people need love and acceptance, meaningful work, and a commitment to something outside themselves to develop self-confidence and feelings of self-worth.

Prejudices

It is natural for children to learn, in part, by placing people and objects into categories. This grouping is one basis of prejudice, when we judge people based on the group to which they belong (ethnic, religious, gender, age, occupation, etc.) rather than the qualities the individual person possesses. Prejudice can be picked up through personal experience, hearsay, rumors, the media, family, and peers. When Dr. Rooney's son was about three years of age he asked his father in a frightened voice, "Dad, there are no white men around here, are there?" When he explored the reason for his son's question it turned out that he had heard a news story in which the reporter told of a bomb being thrown into a school and injuring several children. The reporter concluded with, "A car filled with white men was seen speeding from the scene." After discussing the issue with his son, he said, "Oh, so there are some good white men and some bad ones." This attitudinal and emotional learning occurs at a very early age, although it is modified by subsequent experience.

Just about all of us have some prejudices, even though they vary in degree and intensity. As part of our educational and personal development, we should learn to recognize and overcome our prejudices and help others to do the same.

ACQUIRING LIFE SKILLS

Along with personal and moral development the college years should be a time in which you acquire important life skills. Although these skills aren't taught in the classroom they are essential to functioning as an independent adult.

MANAGING MONEY

One of the purposes of college is to give you the skills to face the kind of challenges you will encounter in your life. One of the most important skills, managing money wisely, is often neglected during the college years.

Most young people learn about economics the way they learn about sex—in bits and pieces from home, from the media, and from their friends. This often adds up to an inadequate education that can have serious consequences for successful living for the rest of their lives. Information you need includes knowledge of student loans, taxes, budgeting, and shopping (including buying or leasing a car and renting or purchasing a house). Most of all, it involves a responsibility in the use of credit. Too many students buy on impulse, run up credit card debt, and end up paying heavy interest in addition to the principal (or incurring the wrath of parents by asking them to foot the bill). Some are consistently late with payments, write checks that bounce, and are negligent or irresponsible in related ways that cause them to be labeled poor credit risks or even to get into legal difficulty.

If you ask young men and women how most people get to be wealthy, you find they have misconceptions as to how this happens. They believe that most millionaires either inherit their wealth or hold high-profile positions like professional athletes or media stars. In reality, most millionaires achieve this level of income by working hard, spending and saving their money wisely, and taking moderate but sensible risks with investments. This path is not as glamorous as becoming a rock star and it doesn't happen overnight. Learning to manage your money at a young age—sticking to a budget (however small), having a savings plan (however little), and using credit wisely—is a habit that will pay off in the long run.

DEALING WITH OVER-INVOLVED PARENTS

Every August, as a new class of freshmen move into the dorms, there are the usual problematic scenarios involving roommates, meal plans, and, especially, final registration for classes. However, another problem has arisen in the last decade. Over-involved parents who seem to be hovering over their child. They have been dubbed "helicopter parents."

College administrators are besieged by aggressive moms and dads who attend campus orientations designed for students only. Parents intrude in the registration process and in students' dealings with professors and administrators more than ever before. Some schools are forced to assign full-time administrative staff or have created new positions simply to deal with parents. *The Wall Street Journal* reports that the University of Vermont employs "parent bouncers," students whose job it is to divert parents who want to attend course registration. Furthermore, it is not uncommon for students, during the registration process, to speed-dial their parents and hand the phone to the faculty or administrative advisor. Richard Mullendore, vice-president of student affairs at the University of Georgia, has labeled the cell phone as "the world's longest umbilical cord."

Students can benefit from parental interest and assistance, but when parents dominate the decision-making process, it denies the first-year student the opportunity to grow as an individual. Partly because of this situation, some administrators have noted that many college freshmen lack the independence and life skills needed to thrive in their new collegiate environment.

FINDING YOUR PERSONAL HIGHWAY

Psychiatrist David D. Burns, author of the bestseller *Feeling Good: The New Mood Therapy,* recommends:

> Aim for success not perfection . . . Remember that fear always lurks behind perfectionism. Confronting your fears and allowing yourself to be human can, paradoxically, make you a far happier and more productive person.

It is not uncommon for some students to be driven to pursue perfection, as measured by the grade point average (GPA). Succinctly stated, the overachiever often has inner demons that generate a stressful lifestyle while achieving academic success. The question that must be addressed is: What price are you willing to pay? The cost/benefit ratio between constant stress and academic success must be examined.

The young man or woman typically has had superior grades since the first grade. This "A" grade fixation becomes an obsession. Early success creates a perspective that only superior performance is acceptable. Like an insidious virus, this belief spreads throughout the thought process over the years. Somehow an "A-" grade or a "B+" (both of which are good grades) is interpreted as failure. Like many other emotional or mental disorders, the student is unable to help himself or herself, but is trapped "inside the box." The stress created by this all-or-nothing mind-set can be deadly. Clearly, such mental health issues must be addressed. A priceless lesson can be learned. Life is not all "A" grades!

Do not allow fear of failure to prevent you from finding your personal highway in your journey through life.

Life Away from Home

Life away from home for the first time is scary and is usually a period of anxiety for the 18-year-old. Below is a list of ideas that may help in this transitional time of your life.

- Do not come home from college on the weekends for at least one month.

- If you can afford it, do not get a job in the first semester (work-study jobs on campus are not included in the statement).

- Do not room with a friend from high school.

- Do discuss with your new roommate the rules of the room.

- Be prepared to have some problems with your roommate's habits and behavior.

- Avoid the use of credit cards if possible.

- Bring prescription medicines, spare eyeglasses, and a cell phone.

- Don't use your roommate's toothpaste or other toiletries. Buy your own when needed.

- Do not ever sit on your roommate's bed. Respect your roommate's space.

- Maintain a weekly visitation schedule with your advising professor.

- Develop a cash fund with your roommate to buy snacks for the room.

- Avoid the Thursday night party atmosphere in the dorm or at local bars.

- Bring a computer that is appropriate for your needs.

- In fall and spring breaks, leave most of your stuff at school.

- Decide with your roommate on the basic standards for keeping the dorm room clean. Perhaps have a rotation system for vacuuming.

Chapter 9

A Safe and Healthy College Experience

The first wealth is health.

—*Ralph Waldo Emerson, "Power," in* The Conduct of Life

As you get ready to leave for college, your parents will be concerned about how you will get along there, including whether you will be safe. Young people often feel invulnerable, and parents worry that they may not take proper precautions in their new environment. Excessive concerns are usually unwarranted, for students in college are generally safe and healthy. Learning to develop a healthy lifestyle during the college years is one of the most important lessons you can learn for your future success and well-being. Unfortunately, too many young people ignore this aspect of their development and regret it later in their lives.

ACCIDENTS

By far the greatest danger to college students is automobile accidents, and by far the greatest contributor to such accidents is alcohol. Other drugs, lack of sleep, and reckless driving are often involved, as well. We recall a student who was noted for driving at speeds that raised the hair on his passengers' heads. His response to pleas to slow down was "I've never had an accident yet." Another student shot back, "You'll never have more than one."

The rule is simple: never drive when you have been drinking, and never ride with a driver who is not completely sober and responsible. If you are going out to a place where you will be drinking, appoint a designated driver who does not drink, take a cab or bus, or rent a limo. There are, of course, other hazards to excessive drinking, but accidents are more likely to be serious or even fatal. Failure to wear a seatbelt adds to the risk. Motorcycles, which provide less protection, a greater need for precaution, and a greater temptation for speeding than cars, are even more hazardous. Biking, skateboarding, rollerblading, and jogging are enjoyable activities, but should be practiced in appropriate places, not amid heavy automobile traffic. Many athletic and recreational activities such as skiing, rock climbing, skydiving, and water sports have an element of risk. Proper instruction and equipment can reduce this risk to the minimum.

INFECTIOUS DISEASE

First-year students living in dorms have an increased risk of contracting meningitis, flu, mononucleosis, and other infectious diseases as they move from living at home to living and interacting with large numbers of fellow students. Each year, an average of more than 100 cases of meningitis occur on college campuses, resulting in about a dozen deaths. In the late 1990s, colleges were confronted with the reality that meningitis was growing in the campus life. In 1998, *The Pendulum,* Elon College's student newspaper, provided an in-depth article on the impact of the disease, including deaths. At that time, the American College Health Association strongly supported the vaccinations that had been approved by the U.S. Food and Drug Administration. It is currently recommended that before starting college, students undergo a physical checkup—including getting any appropriate vaccinations.

Having health insurance coverage during college is a must in the event you require medical treatment or hospitalization. Maintaining good health habits and utilizing student health services will help minimize the risk from infectious diseases. Unfortunately, some students ignore basic standards of sanitation, food storage, and cleanliness. After seeing the conditions under which some students live, one visitor remarked: "Diseases that medical science has labored years to conquer are liable to gain a new foothold here."

Most colleges have considered the possibility of a pandemic that would require the closing of schools for a significant period of time.

Students should be aware of the procedures that faculty have developed to permit them to continue to learn the course material while working on their own if this should occur.

FIRE SAFETY

From time to time, serious fires rage in college residence facilities. In 2000, three students were killed and 58 injured in a widely publicized fire at Seton Hall University in South Orange, New Jersey. Other cases of less serious fires also have occurred, in which there was damage and loss of property, but no casualties. Between 2000 and 2008 there have been 116 campus-related fire fatalities, most of them in off-campus housing.

Older sorority and fraternity houses and other off-campus residences often lack features required for fire safety, either because they are not up to current fire codes or because the codes are inadequate. High-rise dormitories, especially those lacking sprinkler systems, are also particularly vulnerable.

Students sometimes ignore basic precautions, even "borrowing" batteries from dormitory smoke alarms or disabling them as a nuisance. Using candles in dorms can be hazardous, as can bringing in high-wattage appliances that can overload the circuits in dorms and spark electrical fires. In making living arrangements at college, be sure to include fire safety as one priority.

COLLEGE CRIME

As mentioned in Chapter 5, colleges are required by the Clery Act to keep records of crimes that occur on or adjacent to the campus. Some of these incidents are committed by fellow students, some by habitual criminals who target colleges, often traveling long distances and striking a wide number of institutions. You should learn to take sensible precautions with your valuables and with yourself. You may leave your wallet sitting on a table many times without it being taken, but at some time, it will be gone. Develop a sense of alertness to situations that have the smell of danger and avoid them. Your gut reaction to potential danger is a valuable trait to develop and might one day save your life. Certain areas or establishments may be unsafe in general; others may be perfectly safe at 3:00 P.M., but hazardous at 3:00 A.M.

HEALTH HABITS

Develop good health habits during college! This is great preparation for the rest of your life. Admittedly, some students improve these habits after college, but many have become addicted or habituated to nicotine, alcohol, or other drugs, or to overeating, eating junk food, avoiding exercise, failing to get enough regular sleep, or becoming involved sexually in unhealthy ways. Today, most colleges have programs to provide you with information and assistance to help with your physical and mental health. These resources are worth utilizing to make college a more successful experience, and to prepare for a successful life after college.

Exercise

An important part of your personal development is a schedule of regular exercise. It should include aerobic activities such as jogging, swimming, or basketball; a series of stretching exercises; and activities to build muscle tone, such as weight lifting or rock climbing. Most colleges have fitness centers and personal coaches to help you plan workouts in keeping with your current condition and goals. Find a partner or a group to work with and help one another. Make it a social occasion. Pick activities that you enjoy, because that will help you to stick with them. Remember: Fitness is not just for athletes; it's for everyone.

Sleep Deprivation

College students are one of the most sleep-deprived groups in the nation. Long hours of activity and wildly irregular schedules and lifestyles contribute to this. Some observers believe that sleep deprivation contributes to serious accidents as much as alcohol. We all know of students who have dozed off while driving, at times with fatal consequences. Lack of sleep also affects academic performance, feeling of well-being, and general health. It is difficult to concentrate or to approach tasks with enthusiasm when you are drowsy. Why are so many college students sleep deprived? Researchers write that the problem begins in the teens for all young people, students or not. For the college student, a lack of sleep inhibits the learning process. The immune system, motor skills, and intellectual comprehension also are negatively affected.

It is suggested by the research that students need eight hours of sleep to sustain learning capabilities. Few students are sleeping nearly the required amount. The problem is exacerbated when study requirements, part-time jobs, social life, and family obligations are factored into the equation.

Overeating

One of the expressions unique to living in the dorms is the infamous "freshman 15." This is the weight gain common for freshmen, especially for women. Of course, this gain is not inevitable. Recognizing the usual causes can help control it. Here are some factors to note:

- Students tend to eat fast foods, especially those high in fat content.

- Late-night pizza, a vehicle for social interaction in the dorms, often becomes a habit.

- Accessibility to vending machines and fast-food restaurants are common.

- Emotional stress generates a need to feel better. For many students, food high in fat or sugar is the answer.

- Student schedules are often erratic, without set times for eating and exercise. As a result, students eat more and exercise less. Ann Selkowitz Litt's book, *The College Student's Guide to Eating Well* on Campus, emphasizes the concept you are what you eat.

The impact of your diet manifests itself in many ways, mentally, physically, and most importantly, emotionally.

The key to coping with weight problems is exercise on a daily systematic basis. One does not have to go to the weight room or the track. It is as simple as walking briskly for two miles at least six days a week. Obviously, there will be times when you will find excuses not to walk. To overcome this roadblock, make a commitment with two or three friends to walk as a group. This informal contract will obligate you to keep the date. Persistent exercise guarantees weight loss if you monitor your eating habits as you fulfill the exercise routine. If you fall, get back up and continue to put one foot in front of the other. The goal is attainable and very, very important.

It also helps to develop your own schedule with regular times for meals and exercise. Pairing with a friend or a group can help you persist with your exercise regimen and make it a social occasion. Learning about nutrition can help you develop good eating habits.

Students with Disabilities

If you have a disability and you require assistance or special accommodations to enable you to get the most out of your college experience, be sure to notify the appropriate administrative office in advance. A thorough evaluation of your strengths and limitations, and of the kinds of accommodations or other assistance that will help you in meeting college requirements, can be extremely useful here.

Even a minor disability may interfere with your progress, so take advantage of resources that are available, and do your utmost to look after your health and well-being. It is amazing how much students with disabilities can accomplish with the right type of help.

SEXUALITY

Although some young people decide to refrain from sexual intimacy for religious, health, or other reasons, many students are sexually active during their college years. You should know appropriate precautions to take, how to avoid unwanted sexual advances (including how to respond to peer pressure), and how to engage in sexual intimacy with relative safety.

The most serious danger involving sexual behavior is rape, and the most likely kind of rape is acquaintance or date rape. Usually, alcohol or other drugs are involved on the part of one or both parties, and their use (or abuse) increases the risk of date rape. Educational and advocacy programs to prevent or reduce this kind of crime are common on most campuses, and a large number of both men and women are actively involved in them. They are aimed at potential perpetrators as well as possible victims, since those who commit rape often believe they are engaging in consensual sex, or they act on impulse without thinking of the serious consequences. Such programs also provide support for students who report being raped, since victims are often hesitant to bring charges for fear of the stress and embarrassment involved. Some women do not even realize that being forced to have sex with someone they know is really rape. Although heterosexual rape is the most common, homosexual rape does occur. Students should be aware of this possibility, and take appropriate precautions.

Other kinds of sexual misconduct include sexual assault, sexual harassment, and sexual exploitation. Sexual assault involves any intentional sexual touching without effective consent; sexual harassment includes any unwelcome sexual advances, either physical or verbal, and any intimidation or retaliation to deter a person from reporting it; sexual exploitation consists of any act of a sexual nature which places a person in a degrading or humiliating position, for example circulating a nude photo of her or him.

Sexually transmitted diseases are hazards, particularly the danger of contracting AIDS. According to the Centers for Disease Control and Prevention (CDC), nearly a million people in the United States have been infected with HIV, and about 500,000 have died. Across the globe, the incidence of HIV/AIDS is still increasing, with devastating consequences. Moreover, while HIV/AIDS is the most catastrophic, and most widely publicized of the sexually transmitted diseases, a wide variety of other such diseases also can have serious consequences. Unfortunately, students often have misinformation about strategies, aside from sexual abstinence, for minimizing the risk of contracting sexually transmitted diseases. College health centers have accurate information and programs to distribute it. Sexually transmitted diseases (STDs) are transmitted through sexual contact whether oral, vaginal, or anal. Any contact when bodily fluids (blood, semen) are exchanged can lead to an STD.

As an example, at Louisiana State University, 25 percent of students treated in the Student Health Center are treated for a sexually transmitted disease (STD), as reported in the student newspaper. (The CDC's Web site indicates that this rate is roughly applicable to college students across the United States. The most common STDs are human papilloma virus (HPV), genital warts, chlamydia, gonorrhea, and genital herpes.)

Unwanted pregnancies are not uncommon during the college years. The consequences for the woman are obvious, but the man involved may experience serious emotional and financial consequences, as well. Most campus health centers can provide information on preventing both unwanted pregnancies and STDs. However, it is a part of emotional maturity on the student's part to make the effort to be informed about and able to deal with these issues.

RELATIONSHIPS

Falling in love can be a wonderful experience. It has been celebrated throughout the ages in story and song. At times, however, being in love is an emotional roller coaster. And when lovers break up, the emotional upheaval can dominate the person's life for some time. Breakups can trigger depression, feelings of worthlessness, anger, and an inability to concentrate or think straight. It is often so much of a blow to one's ego to be "dumped" that the fear of it happening leads some people to do the dumping first.

A healthy relationship combines a sense of self-worth and reasonable independence with affection and mutual concern. Relationships of this kind are a normal part of healthy social and emotional development. You should feel free to be yourself and to communicate your boundaries when it comes to intimacy. If you break up, you can still like and respect one another.

Many college romances, unfortunately, consist of an excessive emotional dependence on the part of one or both parties. Rather than experiencing the normal disagreements that are present in any relationship and working them through, there is a constant state of frustration that diminishes feelings of self-worth. These relationships can be looked on as "addictive" in that the person knows they are in a bad relationship but seems unable to get out of it. The thought of breaking up generates feeling of anxiety and dependence. This makes it difficult to develop self-determination and to move on with the normal activities needed for personal and career development. Such relationships may even be emotionally abusive in that one partner is belittled, made the butt of jokes, or otherwise degraded by the other. This kind of abuse can be damaging in different ways than physical abuse, but neither should be tolerated.

Other relationships that bear mentioning are rather casual pairing off or "hooking up." Depending on the definition of the persons involved, a hookup can include varying degrees of intimacy up to and including sex. Clear communication is essential to ensure that each person's emotional and physical boundaries are recognized and respected.

MENTAL HEALTH

College students are not immune to emotional problems. In fact, the degree of anxiety, insecurity, depression, sleep disorders, eating disorders, impulsive behavior, anger, and other kinds of emotional upheaval seem to be increasing. Such conditions vary widely in severity, from relatively minor transient incidents that temporarily interfere with academic performance, social relationships, and other kinds of normal activities, to the more serious conditions involving a breakdown of functioning. They may even lead to suicidal behavior, which is the second leading cause of death and is expected to be responsible for 1,100 deaths among those in college this year. There are no completely accurate statistics on suicide rate among college students, but it is usually reported as somewhat lower than for members of the same age group who are not in college. A 2006 National Survey of College Counseling Center Directors reported 142 suicides. Although this survey includes only a portion of colleges, the figure is notably lower than reported in past years by the same survey. This suggests that efforts to prevent suicide are becoming more effective.

Of directors responding, 92 percent believe that the number of students with severe psychological problems has increased in recent years. In the past year, for example, 2,368 students were hospitalized with psychological problems. They also reported 466 cases of obsessive pursuit, with 124 students being injured and 10 killed by the pursuer.

Fortunately, colleges have facilities and support systems to help treat and prevent emotional problems, and they tend to be relatively effective.

Stress is a normal part of life, and if not excessive, can be a motivator to help us accomplish goals. When stress becomes excessive, however, it interferes with our performance and can be detrimental to our health. The first step in dealing with stress is to learn to recognize its signs. While they vary somewhat from person to person, such characteristics as rapid heart beat, sweaty palms, and tension in various muscles are common indicators of stress. Next, it helps to know what is causing the stress. It may be time pressure, fear of failure, concerns about possible rejection, or a variety of other possibilities. Knowing the cause can help you prevent or control it. Practices for controlling excessive stress, like meditation, progressive relaxation, yoga, and tai chi are helpful, as is regular exercise, particularly walking and swimming.

Students, like the public at large, are increasingly recognizing the value of regularly consulting a professional counselor, or other mental health professional, not only as a way of treating or helping to prevent problems, but as a means of enhancing development. Students can also support one another in fostering a healthy lifestyle and in seeking professional help. Campuses have mental health workers who can help you make the most of your college years and maybe even save your life.

BODY IMAGE

The media and the fashion industry put considerable emphasis on body image. To develop your awareness of how much you are influenced by this characteristic, ask yourself how you judge your friends and people you admire. Do most of them conform to a certain body image, or do they vary in body type? Are there qualities that you like about them that have nothing to do with body image? If you find that you are, in fact, admiring or rejecting people based largely on whether they fit a certain body type, this is a warning sign to stop and recheck your values. Not only are you judging people by superficial characteristics, but you are missing out on the chance to get to know many wonderful people who don't happen to fit the "ideal" image.

Of course, it is natural to want to look good and to have people like us. We often find, however, that while students judge others based on a variety of qualities, not mainly body image, they believe others are judging them mainly by appearance. Large numbers of men, and even larger numbers of women, are dissatisfied by the way they look. For women, the ideal is "the thinner the better" so that even those who are already slender diet and exercise to get thinner yet. Women of normal weight often consider themselves to be too heavy.

Women may find themselves looking for "miracle diets" or weight-loss drugs, or in other ways focusing too much time and energy on achieving an ideal body image. Some men also become obsessed with thinness, often developing an addiction to running long distances and eating sparsely. More commonly, the ideal male body image emphasizes muscle bulk, and the male obsession is with bulking up. This becomes a problem when men find themselves putting excess time in a fitness center, postponing doing things that are important until they have developed a better build, and taking more vitamins, herbal supplements, or other drugs than is good for their health.

Eating Disorders

Excessive concern about body image can lead to eating disorders. These vary in severity from relatively minor to those that are life threatening. Most common is a preoccupation with food, concerns about how much you have eaten, how you can make it up, how to cut down, and how you can look better. This can come to dominate a person's thinking.

Knowing the signs of eating disorders can help you avoid them or recognize when you need counseling. You can also help any friends who show symptoms of an eating disorder by telling them of your concerns and encouraging them to seek professional assistance.

Anorexia Nervosa

This disorder involves such a concern over weight that the person diets excessively. Even after experiencing significant weight loss, the person (it is more common among women) continues to believe that he or she is not thin enough and restricts food intake accordingly. Symptoms include dry skin and hair, cold hands and feet, weakness and digestive disorders. Women with this disorder stop menstruating. If anorexia nervosa persists, it can be fatal.

Bulimia

In this disorder, the person goes on frequent eating binges accompanied by some kind of compensatory behavior so as not to gain weight (laxatives, vomiting, or excessive exercise). People with bulimia (also called bulimia nervosa) are hypercritical of their body image. Bulimia can lead to habitual unintentional vomiting, decayed teeth, electrolyte imbalance, and damage to the esophagus, including esophageal cancer later in life.

Binge Eating Disorder

In this disorder, the person binges on food a couple of times a week and persists in this behavior for several months but without accompanying compensatory behavior. This leads to being overweight, and even obesity, often accompanied by high blood pressure, shortness of breath and joint problems.

DRUG AND ALCOHOL USE AT COLLEGE

America has been called a drug culture. We have been conditioned, by advertising and the example of other people, to look to drugs to change our lives and solve our problems. To relieve pain, sleep better, stay awake, reduce tension, have more energy and more fun, or enhance our performance, we are told that some kind of drug is the answer. Advertisers for alcohol, as well as over-the-counter and prescription drugs, spend millions of dollars each year.

Some medication is useful, of course, if taken under appropriate supervision. Too many people, however, take too much over too long a period of time and combine too many drugs without considering possible adverse reactions that can occur. One of the most common kinds of poisoning today occurs from taking too much aspirin, Tylenol, or other over-the-counter pain relievers. Young people often foolishly experiment with drugs that have been prescribed for their parents or other relatives or friends.

If prescription and over-the-counter drugs are a problem (and they are, in fact, a major one), using illegal or street drugs is an even more serious one. In addition to the danger inherent in the drug itself and the possibility of criminal penalties, they pose the problem of usually containing other substances with potential for harm. Those who experiment with drugs often try more than one type and frequently do not know what drug or what strength they are taking. In addition to the physical and mental problems associated with drugs, their use commonly contributes to social, financial, and legal difficulties.

College-age youth are inclined to try new experiences and are often tempted to experiment with drugs. A wide variety of drugs are available in high schools and colleges, and most students have access to them; yet, they are generally aware that there are problems associated with using them. The most widely used drugs in college are caffeine, alcohol, and nicotine. Marijuana, although avoided by the majority of students, is popular with a fair-sized minority. Most other illegal drugs are used by only a small percentage of students, but even that number is enough to cause significant concerns for parents and fellow students, as well as faculty and staff. All students should be familiar with the effects of these drugs as a part of their education. They should also be able to recognize signs of drug problems in fellow students and help them get help.

Nicotine

One of the most widespread and most dangerous drugs is nicotine. Anyone who has seen the suffering of a loved one dying from lung cancer or another tobacco-related illnesses should be able to understand how upsetting it can be to see bright, healthy, attractive young people taking up smoking. It is much easier to avoid smoking in the first place than it is to quit once you have become addicted. An increasing number of college students are avoiding or breaking the tobacco habit, not only for their own future, but to set an example for family and friends. The prevalence of daily smoking among college students is now down to 12 percent versus 28 percent of their age group who are not attending college full time.

Generally, the most deadly consequences of smoking lie in the future, but there are some immediate benefits of not smoking. You usually feel better and have better athletic performance; you don't see your spending money go up in smoke; your breath, clothes, hair, and bedroom do not have the stench of stale cigarettes; you don't annoy other students who are concerned about the effects of secondhand smoke; and you are not a potential fire hazard. If you set goals for yourself while you are starting college, quitting or not taking up smoking should be high on your list.

A relatively new fad among some high school and college students is the use of the hookah or water pipe. Long a Middle-Eastern practice, it has been taken up by some young people as a hip or fashionable way of smoking flavored tobacco. It is just as dangerous to your health as any other smoking method despite the widespread belief that it is safer.

Caffeine

A student came in for counseling because he was very nervous and jittery and had trouble sleeping. After some questioning, he mentioned that he drank several liter bottles of cola every night. There was then no mystery about the cause of these symptoms.

Most people are affected by this stimulant, some more than others. It is found in many foods, including coffee (in its many forms), tea, soft drinks, and chocolate. Students often give little thought to the amount of caffeine they ingest, but excessive caffeine intake is a common problem.

Alcohol

Alcohol is the most widely used and most dangerous drug on college campuses. According to recent national statistics, the greatest incidence of problem drinking occurs in 18- to 25-year-olds. It is the one drug that college students use more frequently than their contemporaries who do not attend college, with 68 percent reporting alcohol consumption in the past 30 days, versus 59 percent of those not in college. According to a 2006 study, students also had a higher rate of incidents of heavy drinking—defined in the study as five or more drinks in a row—in the past two weeks (40 percent versus 35 percent). Fatalities linked directly to alcohol use by students now number more than 1,700 a year. Alcohol consumption is involved in the rape or sexual assault of 70,000 college students per year, and in the physical assault of 600,000. Excessive drinking, particularly binge drinking, has other consequences, including failing courses and dropping out of college.

Alcohol consumption is also expensive. College students spend approximately two billion dollars per year on beer alone. No wonder money for recreation is often referred to as "beer money."

Elaine Pasqua, an educator and expert on collegiate alcohol abuse, makes presentations to colleges across the nation relating to the problem. Whether alcohol is used as an inhibition release or a pseudo-confidence builder, its use can become a debilitating and destructive disease that can destroy lives: alcohol abuse has been tied to date rape, suicide, and drug addiction. Pasqua states, "300 college students die from alcohol poisoning, and 1,400 die from alcohol-related accidents annually." Furthermore, drinking is often the catalyst for unprotected sex, a fact punctuated by a particular CDC statistic: 1 out of 4 college students has a sexually transmitted disease.

Ultimately, you must accept the responsibility for the lifestyle you adopt in college. Maturation, self-esteem, and courage are needed to stand fast against the inevitable peer pressure you will encounter. As much as parents try to instill appropriate values, the buck stops with you. It is incumbent upon you to resist the pressure to conform to a behavior pattern that is dangerous.

To be able to "just say no," under various circumstances, is essential for your success. Many students decide not to drink at all; many others are able to exercise moderation. Obviously, the more developed, independent, and mature you are, the less likely you are to suffer the consequences of alcohol abuse in trying to achieve peer acceptance. It is important to develop problem-solving and stress-coping skills, so there is no need for artificial stimulation.

Recently, the incidence of problem drinking among young women has exceeded that of their male counterparts. It is important for women to be aware that they are more susceptible to alcohol than men, and to refrain from or moderate their drinking accordingly.

Students often come up with rationalizations for drinking, such as "It relaxes me," "I'm more fun when I drink," and "It helps me to study."

In 1999, Harvard University's School of Public Health conducted research on alcohol use by students at 119 colleges. The binge drinker was over 20 times more likely than non-binge drinkers to have:

- Missed class

- Fallen behind in class work

- Damaged property

- Been injured

- Engaged in unsafe sex

- Gotten in trouble with campus police

- Been cited for drunkenness

According to this same survey the primary reasons for drinking were:

- To get drunk

- To achieve status associated with drinking

- To be part of the campus culture

- To address peer pressure and academic stress

It may seem odd that a student facing pressure from a term paper or exam would seek to escape from the pressure by getting drunk rather than facing up to the job and getting it done. Yet escaping stress and responsibility is a common trigger for drinking. This pattern may persist for life.

Students in one of Dr. Rooney's classes wrote a paper describing approaches they found useful in avoiding excessive drinking. Some of their points:

- Learn not to be influenced by advertising that identifies social acceptance or having a good time with drinking.

- Don't associate alcohol with a reward. Be able to work hard without thinking that you deserve a drink for your efforts.

- Switch to something nonalcoholic when you have had enough and well before you have had too much.

- Don't pool your money with others in buying drinks. Avoid being in the position of wanting to get your money's worth.

- Quench your thirst with water before taking alcoholic drinks. Take your time. Drink slowly. Keep a full drink in your hand for a long time.

- Never leave a drink unattended (alcoholic or nonalcoholic). Never drink anything that you have not opened yourself. (These two tips help keep others from tampering with your drinks).

- Never drive after drinking. Make alternate plans.

A DANGEROUS FAD

A recent fad involves inhaling alcohol as fumes from a humidifier rather than drinking it, in an attempt to get the high without the calories. It has the same dangers as drinking (and perhaps some we have not yet uncovered). It is clearly more difficult to know how much you are consuming and thus guard against overdoing it.

- Never assume that other people will take care of you if you drink too much. Take care of yourself by drinking in moderation or not at all.

- Know the alcohol content of what you are drinking and the amount. Some brands of beer, wine, and whiskey have twice the alcohol of others. And one six-ounce glass of wine is obviously the same as two three-ounce glasses. Mixed drinks vary even more widely in the amount of alcohol they contain, so approach with caution.

A number of universities have substance-free housing available for students who prefer to live in a residence where there is no alcohol or other drugs. This is a wise choice.

Marijuana

Marijuana, in addition to being an illegal drug, is a contributor to accidents, leads to indifference to studies, and has health hazards similar to cigarettes. About one-third of high school seniors have tried it, and about 5 percent of them use it daily. The incidence of use has increased in recent years. Between 1992 and 2005, past-month use has increased from 12 percent to 20 percent among high school seniors.

In college, as in high school, it continues to be the most commonly used illicit drug, although the incidence of use varies considerably from one college to another. One subculture within most colleges uses it regularly at parties, and some students fall into the habit of using it every day. A 2005 national survey reported by the University of Michigan found that 4 percent of college students reported using it daily, 17 percent within the previous month, and 33 percent within the past year.

Marijuana usually produces euphoria, decreased inhibitions, and disorientation. Students who are frequent users typically develop an indifference to studies and other responsibilities. Despite popular notions to the contrary, it interferes with the ability to drive and to perform other skilled tasks.

Both the use and distribution of marijuana are illegal, although there continue to be some efforts to legalize or decriminalize the drug. Students who believe that violations of laws regarding marijuana will be winked at or minimized by authorities (as they sometimes are) are often rudely surprised when they encounter places or situations where harsh sentences are meted out for what, to the student, seems like a minor violation.

Sometimes other substances (often unknown to the user) are mixed with marijuana, including crack cocaine, PCP, and embalming fluid. Approximately 120,000 people are admitted to emergency rooms and 220,000 enter drug treatment each year with marijuana use as their primary problem. Hashish, like marijuana, is derived from the cannabis (hemp) plant and has similar effects.

Other Illegal Drugs

The percentage of college students that uses drugs other than alcohol and marijuana is relatively small. Yet, in a university of 20,000 students, even 2 percent of this group using an illicit drug would amount to 400 students. Thus, it is helpful to be aware of the way drugs affect people, so you can recognize their impact on other students and be able to help them. Knowledge should also help you avoid becoming involved with such drugs.

Barbiturates and Tranquilizers

Barbiturates (such as Phenobarbital) and tranquilizers (such as Valium) are depressants, like alcohol. They reduce tension, depress reflexes, and impair motor function. When taken in excess, they cause rapid pulse, shallow breathing, coma, and possibly death.

Among college students, 2.2 percent report using tranquilizers and 1.3 percent using barbiturates in the past 30 days.

Opiates

Opiates are narcotics, depressants or "downers," which are derived from the opium poppy or produced synthetically. Morphine, heroin, opium, and codeine are common forms. They relieve pain, produce drowsiness and euphoria, and impair cognitive functioning. An overdose causes slow shallow breathing, nausea, convulsions, coma, and possibly death. Tolerance and addiction develop quickly, and withdrawal is difficult. About 15 percent of those in treatment for drug abuse are addicted to heroin. Among college students, 0.1 percent report using heroin and 3.1 percent report using other narcotics within the past month.

Cocaine

Cocaine is a stimulant, or "upper," which produces alertness, excitation, euphoria, and sleeplessness. It may be sniffed, injected, or smoked (crack cocaine). An overdose causes agitation, paranoid delusions, convulsions, and possibly death. During withdrawal, the user experiences depression, agitation, and sleep disorders. Dependence on the drug develops quickly. In the United States, there are now approximately two million users of this drug.

Among people 18 to 25 years of age, the period of greatest risk for dependence, 15 percent have tried cocaine, but only 1.8 percent of college students report using it in the past month.

Amphetamines and Methamphetamines

Also known as meth, speed, and crank, these stimulants cause feelings of self-confidence, energy, reduced fatigue, reduced hunger, and increased sex drive. They can also produce anxiety, irritability, aggression, and paranoia; there is also the danger of a stroke or heart attack. Despite their danger, these drugs are becoming increasingly prevalent, especially in the Midwest, the South, and on the West Coast. In 2004, Federal agents shut down over 17,000 methamphetamine labs.

Among college students, 3.1 percent report using these drugs in the past 30 days.

Hallucinogens

LSD, PCP, mescaline (peyote), and psilocybin ("magic" mushrooms) are examples of hallucinogens. They produce distortions of reality, changes in time perception, illusions, and hallucinations. In excess, psychotic reactions and death are possibilities. Only 1.3 percent of college students report using hallucinogens in the past 30 days.

Club Drugs

GHB and other club drugs are often abused by young people at all-night parties and "raves," but evidence indicates that GHB abuse is spreading beyond the club scene. For example, bodybuilders have said they use GHB because it stimulates the release of growth hormone. Alcoholics may take GHB in an attempt to eliminate alcohol cravings, in spite of a lack of medical approval for this use in the United States. (In some European countries, GHB is prescribed as a treatment for alcoholism.)

GHB is most often abused in an attempt to feel euphoric, relaxed, and uninhibited. In the United States, GHB can be prescribed in a very low dose as an experimental treatment for narcolepsy, a sleep disorder, under tightly controlled conditions. However, those who abuse GHB (also known as "G" or "liquid ecstasy") may require emergency medical attention when they overdose or experience withdrawal symptoms.

MDMA is a synthetic, psychoactive drug with both stimulant (amphetamine-like) and hallucinogenic (LSD-like) properties. Only 0.8 percent of college students report using MDMA in the past month. MDMA is also neurotoxic. In addition, in high doses it can cause a sharp increase in body temperature (malignant hyperthermia), leading to muscle breakdown and kidney and cardiovascular system failure.

Ketamine is a central nervous system depressant that produces a rapid-acting dissociative effect. It was developed in the 1970s as an anesthetic for both humans and animals. Ketamine is often mistaken for cocaine or crystal methamphetamine because of a similarity in appearance.

It is available in tablet, powder, and liquid form. So powerful is the drug that, when injected, there is a risk of losing motor control before the injection is completed. In powder form, the drug can be snorted or sprinkled on tobacco or marijuana and smoked. The effects of ketamine last from one to six hours, and it is usually 24 to 48 hours before the user feels completely "normal" again.

DRUG DANGERS

All kinds of over-the-counter, prescription, and illegal or "street drugs" are available on college campuses. There are always new fads in drugs and rediscoveries of once-popular old drugs. There are always deaths and adverse reactions from accidental overdoses. The general rule: Don't experiment with drugs "just to see what they are like." You can't be sure what harm a drug may do. Nor can you tell what the strength is of an illegally produced drug. And one trial may be one too many. Also, don't take prescription drugs from other people; use only what your physician has prescribed or recommended for you.

You should also be aware of the possibility of someone slipping drugs into your drink, be it alcoholic or nonalcoholic. They may also be added to or substituted for other drugs. The reasons for this vary. The sexual predator may use date rape drugs such as Rohypnol (roofies), Gamma-hydroxybutyrate acid (GHB), or ketamine. These cause a sleep-like behavior and a kind of amnesia. Alcohol, if present, increases the effect. In one instance, a young woman who was staying in a hotel on a business trip stopped in the bar for one drink. She soon found herself semiconscious and being dragged to a car by two strangers. She was able to call for help, and the hotel doorman and a passerby managed to free her. Tests at the hospital showed the clear presence of a date rape drug.

There are cards and coasters that test for such drugs by changing colors, but they are not completely accurate and don't work at all with some drugs. The "practical joker" gets his or her kicks from seeing what kind of embarrassing things you might do under the drug's influence, perhaps even videotaping your antics and displaying them on the Web.

SUMMARY

Proper attention to nutrition and hygiene, regular hours of sleep, study, exercise, and recreation will not only help ensure success in college, but will stand you in good stead for the rest of your life. For, if college is preparation for life, experience indicates that a well-balanced lifestyle is one of the keys to success and satisfaction.

Chapter 10

The Role of Inspiration and Commitment

Even if you are on the right track, you'll get run over if you just sit there.

—Will Rogers

Imagination is more important than knowledge.

—Albert Einstein

Curiosity and passion are more important than IQ.

—Thomas L. Friedman, The World Is Flat

Dream the impossible . . . then live so that dream is fulfilled.

—Maired Maguire, The Vision of Peace

The intellectual is constantly betrayed by his vanity. God-like, he blandly assumes that he can express everything in words; whereas the things one lives, loves and dies for are not, in the last analysis, completely expressible in words.

—Anne Morrow Lindbergh

As the above quotations indicate, what we as authors can provide in a book is limited. Factual information, suggestions, and the experience of others can all be useful to the student preparing for college. Yet what gives meaning and zest to life is the passion and commitment with which it is pursued. Each of us must find our own sources of inspiration and direction. We, the authors, have included in this chapter a sample of things that, in some way, have touched us. We include them in the hope that they may also have value for you.

THE EXPERIENCE OF OTHERS

Dr. Rooney recalls the first time he was preparing for a trip overseas. It was to London, and friends were giving him things to help him get ready: lists of restaurants, shops, and historical sites; pamphlets, maps, and guides; a few British coins; even a roll of American toilet tissue. Most valued of all, however, was a book a friend recommended entitled *London, the Civilized City.* Reading it in advance piqued his interest, gave him a sense of perspective, and made the actual experience of London so much more meaningful and enjoyable. Likewise, in preparing for college, the experience of others who have been there and done that can help you get more out of your prospective journey.

HISTORICAL PERSPECTIVE

During the 1930s and early 1940s, only 5 percent of the college-age population attended college. In essence, there was not much of a middle class. Immigrants and children of immigrants worked as laborers and most people were poor. Upward mobility, from an economic perspective was nonexistent. And, of course, the Great Depression was the ultimate catastrophe of the 1930s. Following World War II, the number of people attending college increased rapidly, as returning veterans took advantage of the G.I. Bill, which paid for their education.

Yet fewer than 40 percent of high school graduates attended college in the 1950s. With the passage of time and the birth of the community college system in the mid-1960s, that percentage increased. Because of the developing middle class, there was an increase in demand for people to become physicians, lawyers, accountants, and psychologists—just to name a few professions. Hence, a college degree was the ticket into the professional work arena. Women were the last piece of the puzzle needed to complete the collegiate landscape as we presently know it. Prior to that time, most young women in high school focused on typing and stenography with the expectation of becoming secretaries after high school.

As late as the early 1970s, women were not being readily accepted into medical schools or in certain professions, such as accounting and engineering. The expression "the glass ceiling" referred to the subtle limits imposed on women in the business world. It truly existed. The humanities, social sciences, nursing, and, especially education, were the prescribed areas for female students. One example of the prejudice college women encountered was the "witticism" that rather than working for a B.A. or B.S., what they really wanted was a "MRS." Gender prejudice, coupled with ethnic and racial discrimination, was pervasive until the Civil Rights Act was passed in 1964; it has gradually decreased since that date.

Today, almost anyone who graduates from high school and has the desire is able to complete college. The motivation must come from within us, but we can find inspiration from many sources.

SOURCES OF INSPIRATION

In talking with high school and college students about their main source of inspiration, one common answer was one or both parents. Many young women emphasized how much they admired their mothers and yet how they wanted to do more with their own lives because they realized they had more advantages.

In my life (Reardon), education was not a given. My father had only a third-grade education. As the child of Irish immigrants, he, at age 10, went to work in the anthracite coal mines of Pennsylvania. Ten-hour days for 10-year-olds were not uncommon for those desperately poor families.

My father enlisted in the army during World War I. At war's end, there would be no more coal mining in his future. Rather, a 43-year job in a North Philadelphia factory was his escape.

He had decided that I would be the first in our family to be college educated, but at age 15, with some degree of trepidation, I informed my father that I wanted to skip college and make some money. To my surprise, he agreed, and the next day informed me that I had a summer job in his factory. Within a week, I realized that this horrifically exhausting and debilitating job was a living nightmare. Nothing in my life had prepared me for this trauma as I worked next to massive steel ovens in the cellar of a dilapidated and depressing old mill. I sought to end it. I promised to attend college. My father was delighted, but unrelenting on the factory issue. For the next three summers I endured the hellish factory position.

As a first-generation college student, I was on a highway in life that none of my family had ever traveled. Could I achieve academically? Were not these other students brighter than I? Again, my father's wisdom shone through. In his profoundly direct way, he reminded me that none of the other students would outwork me. At least, they better not!

In retrospect, my father taught me many lessons, but the essence of his message was the realization that education is the catalyst for economic freedom. Deprivation builds character; inspiration builds confidence. My father's life was the catalyst for my personal metamorphosis.

Although parental influence on my life (Rooney) was also paramount, other sources of inspiration include Boy Scout leaders, college faculty members, and the few psychologists I encountered, especially one who was an instructor during my naval flight training (he went through the flight program himself so he could appreciate what we were experiencing).

As I reflect on my journey on the highway of life. I realize that inspiration for the pursuit of a college degree was the by-product of many experiences, both external and internal.

My students and my children have also influenced me. For example, when my eldest daughter was in college, she took a part-time job as a recreation director at a school for neglected and dependent youth. A schedule of visits to museums, TV stations, and historic sites had been arranged. After the first few trips supervising these teenagers, in which she found her role mainly controlling their high jinks and horseplay, she decided that they would benefit more from a different experience. She arranged for them to serve as volunteers in a children's hospital, a retirement home, and a rehabilitation unit. They quickly developed a pride in their work and a sense of purpose. They learned that helping others is a sure road to developing a sense of self worth.

Of the many times I have been influenced by a student, I think of one instance in the early days of a pre-college counseling program we had developed. We invited incoming first-year students to come in during the summer to assist them in planning for college. Afterward we surveyed all of the students to see whether they found the experience beneficial.

One of them added a comment to the survey: "What impressed me most about the program was the enthusiasm of the faculty who participated. Don't ever lose your enthusiasm!" It reminded me that, when you approach a task with enthusiasm, you not only enjoy it more, but you generate enthusiasm in others too. I think of Helen Keller's statement, "Alone we can do so little; together we can do so much."

In some circumstances, young people have to look beyond the aspirations of family and friends. The 1999 movie, *October Sky*, captures the pressure on boys growing up in a West Virginia mining town to remain in their town and follow their fathers in working in the mines. Based on actual events, it shows how a few of the boys were able to resist this pressure, become fascinated with rocketry, and go on to become scientists and engineers.

In the book, *Manchild in the Promised Land*, lawyer Claude Brown tells of the appeal of the self-destructive street culture of Harlem in the 1950s. He emphasizes how hard it was to persist with his education and break away from his friends, even though he could see that they would soon be in prison or in the morgue.

THE MAYONNAISE JAR AND THE GOLF BALLS

The following story has made the rounds on the Internet. Its original author is unknown.

A professor stood before his philosophy class and had some items in front of him. When the class began, he wordlessly picked up a large and empty mayonnaise jar and proceeded to fill it with golf balls. He then asked the students if the jar was full. They agreed that it was. The professor then picked up a box of pebbles and poured them into the jar. He shook the jar lightly. The pebbles rolled into the open areas between the golf balls. He then asked the students again if the jar was full. They agreed it was. The professor next picked up a box of sand and poured it into the jar. Of course, the sand filled up everything else. He asked once more if the jar was full. The students responded with a unanimous "Yes." The professor then produced two cups of coffee from under the table and poured the entire contents into the jar, effectively filling the empty space between the sand. The students laughed.

"Now," said the professor as the laughter subsided, "I want you to recognize that this jar represents your life. The golf balls are the important things—God, your family, your children, your health, your friends, and your favorite passions—and if everything else was lost and only they remained, your life would still be full. The pebbles are the other things that matter like your job, your house, and your car. The sand is everything else—the small stuff."

"If you put the sand into the jar first," he continued, "there is no room for the pebbles or the golf balls. The same goes for life. If you spend all your time and energy on the small stuff, you will never have room for the things that are important to you. Pay attention to the things that are critical to your happiness. Play with your children. Spend time with your parents. Visit with grandparents. Take time to get medical checkups. Take your spouse out to dinner. There will always be time to clean the house and fix the disposal. Take care of the golf balls first—the things that really matter. Set your priorities. The rest is just sand."

One of the students raised her hand and inquired what the coffee represented. The professor smiled. "I'm glad you asked. It just goes to show you that no matter how full your life may seem, there's always room for a cup of coffee with a friend."

NEVER GIVE UP

Shortly before his death in January 1965, Winston Churchill, the Prime Minister of England during World War II, gave the commencement address at a university in Great Britain. The great statesman was in poor health at this point in his life. In fact, he was within months of his death. He had to be helped to the podium and he stood there saying nothing for what seemed to be an interminable period of time. Suddenly, that uplifting voice that had once inspired the people of Great Britain to fight back from the edge of defeat, sounded for the last time in public, and what he said was, "Never give up! Never, never, never give up!" After staring at the graduates for close to a minute, he turned and went back to his seat. There was a moment of stunned silence, and then the graduates and guests rose to their feet and passionately generated sustained applause. Historians say it is the only commencement address to be remembered verbatim by everyone who heard it. What made it so moving was that the words were so congruent with the one who said them. Churchill's career had been pronounced dead, again and again, but he continued to return. The prime minister believed that the worst things are never the last things. At times, he became discouraged but he never gave up.

Hopefully, this will be your mantra as you struggle with the frustrations, disappointments, and problems that you will have to confront in your life.

IF I ONLY KNEW IN COLLEGE . . .

Amazingly, we become so much wiser as we age. We reflect upon and then regret so many things that we did or didn't do during the college years. With hindsight, we understand that so much time was wasted. Time-management skills were beyond the capability level of most teenagers. The maturation process was just beginning.

Perhaps the biggest mistake for most young college students is the passionate belief that one is supposed to know what to do with his or her life as graduation looms. Looking back, one can laugh at the absurdness of that concept. We believe that it is not necessary (or crucial) to select the "right" major. In my department (Accounting) an informal survey of the graduates, five or more years after graduation, showed that approximately 50 percent were not working in accounting positions. Simply, the major was a conduit to the first job but not to a career.

You don't have to choose your life's work while in college. Opportunity is down the road, and all you need is a vehicle to transport you in that direction. What you should do is experiment in the hope that you will discover what you like. Did you ever hear the expression that if you love what you do, it is not work?

In this ever-changing world, it is not a good idea to have an inflexible perspective. The only certainty is change. The irony with this is that there will be rewarding careers you can't learn about because, at the moment, they don't yet exist.

At every high school graduation, speakers extol the students to follow their dreams. No one disputes the wisdom of that position, but it creates tremendous stress for the young graduate. It implies that he or she is supposed to be committed to some plan already in place. How demoralizing, when you lack such a conviction. The impact for the vast majority is disaster. "Oh, woe is me, I don't have a plan." Of course not, you are still in your teens. A more substantive piece of advice is, "Never give up and never stop looking." Lastly, never underestimate your potential and your ability. Of course, the difficult part in that equation is discovering what abilities you possess.

When you start college, most departments will look the same. The best scenario is to select a program that has rigor and challenge. You must be challenged if you want to grow intellectually. Challenges faced lead to success and ultimately, exhilaration. You have climbed the mountain!

If you were to ask college graduates with 10 or more years of career experience what they regret most about their college life it is nearly always the same thing: that they wasted so much time. Please, be apprised!

To gain the greatest return on your investment of time and money, you must be focused on the challenges and problems that are a part of this lifestyle. As this process is ongoing, you will be less intimidated and more confident.

EPILOGUE

The theme of this book is that you spend your collegiate life with the belief that the glass is half full rather than half empty. Appreciate all the blessings you have, never forget those less fortunate than you, and always, always do your best.

Appendix: Online Sources for College Planning

The sources listed in this appendix can provide you with up-to-the-minute information and give you a jumping-off point for the many facets of college planning.

General College Planning and Research

CollegeAdmissionInfo.com
http://www.collegeadmissioninfo.com/

The CollegeBoard
http://www.collegeboard.com

College Confidential
http://www.collegeconfidential.com/

College Parents of America
http://www.collegeparents.org/cpa/index.html

CollegeView
http://www.collegeview.com/

CollegeTransfer.net
http://www.collegetransfer.net/
Offers advice and information for students who are transferring to another college.

eCampusTours.com
http://www.ecampustours.com/
Help plan your college visit by taking a virtual tour. Over 1,200 campuses available.

The Princeton Review
http://www.princetonreview.com

U.S. News and World Report: America's Best Colleges 2008
http://colleges.usnews.rankingsandreviews.com/usnews/edu/college/
rankings/rankindex_brief.php

Financial Aid

Athletic Scholarships.net
http://www.athleticscholarships.net/

CollegeScholarships.org
http://www.collegescholarships.org/

FastWeb
http://www.fastweb.com
FastWeb is the Internet's leading scholarship search service.

Federal Work-Study Program
http://www.ed.gov/programs/fws/index.html

FinAid
http://www.finaid.org/

Free Application for Federal Student Aid (FAFSA)
http://www.fafsa.ed.gov/

National Association of Student Financial Aid Administrators
http://www.nasfaa.org

National Merit Scholarship Corporation
http://www.nationalmerit.org/

National Scholarship Service (NSS)
http://www.nssfns.com/
The National Scholarship Service offers free college advisory and refer-
ral service for African American students who plan to attend two-year
or four-year colleges.

NCAA Scholarships

http://www.ncaa.org/about/scholarships/school.html

ROTC

http://www.todaysmilitary.com/before-serving/rotc

SallieMae: Planning and Preparing for School

http://salliemae.com/before_college/

Student Aid on the Web

http://studentaid.ed.gov

Saving for College

http://www.savingforcollege.com/

Scholarships.com

http://www.scholarships.com/

Student Loan Network

http://www.studentloannetwork.com/
The Student Loan Network is one of the United States' largest hubs of student loans and financial aid information.

U.S. Department of Education Grant Programs

http://www.ed.gov/programs/find/title/index.html?src=ov

College Admissions Tests and Test Prep

ACT

http://www.actstudent.org/

AP

http://www.collegeboard.com/student/testing/ap/about.html

Barron's TestPrep

http://www.barronstestprep.com/

CLEP

http://www.collegeboard.com/student/testing/clep/about.html

Kaplan
http://www.kaptest.com/index.jhtml

PSAT/NMSQT
http://www.collegeboard.com/student/testing/psat/about.html

SAT
http://www.collegeboard.com/student/testing/sat/about.html

College Applications

AdmissionsEssays.com
http://www.admissionsessays.com/
This site, featured in the Los Angeles Times, *provides students help with their admissions essays and personal statements.*

The Common Application
https://www.commonapp.org/CommonApp/default.aspx

Essay Edge.com
http://www.essayedge.com/
The New York Times *calls this "the world's premier application essay editing service."*

College Majors, Careers, and Interest Assessment

Americorps
http://www.americorps.org/

GoAbroad.com
http://www.goabroad.com/

InternJobs.com
http://www.internjobs.com/

InternshipPrograms.com
http://www.internshipprograms.com/

Mapping Your Future
http://mappingyourfuture.org/

MyMajors.com
http://www.mymajors.com/index.html

National Commission for Cooperative Education (NCCE)
http://www.co-op.edu/

The Occupational Outlook Handbook, from U.S. Department of Labor
http://www.bls.gov/oco/

The Self-Directed Search
http://www.self-directed-search.com/

The Strong Interest Inventory
http://www.careers-by-design.com/strong_interest_inventory.asp

StudyAbroad.com
http://www.studyabroad.com/

The World-of-Work Map
http://www.act.org/wwm/index.html

Student Issues

American College Health Association
http://www.acha.org/

CampusBlues.com
http://www.campusblues.com/health.asp
Provides information on health, mental health, substance abuse, and other problems faced by college students.

College Freshman
http://www.college-freshman.com/

College Freshmen
http://www.collegefreshmen.net/

GoCollege.com: Free College Survival Guide
http://www.gocollege.com/survival/

HealthyMinds.org
http://www.healthyminds.org/collegementalhealth.cfm

Higher Education Center for Alcohol and Other Drug Abuse and Violence Prevention
http://www.higheredcenter.org/

How to Study
http://www.how-to-study.com/
Expert tips on study skills.

LD Online: College and College Prep
http://www.ldonline.org/indepth/college
Contains information on college preparation and adjustment for students with learning disabilities.

The Nuts and Bolts of College Writing
http://nutsandboltsguide.com/
Tips for writing college papers from a college writing professor.

Security on Campus, Inc.
http://www.securityoncampus.org/
Information on campus crime and security, including background on the Clery Act.

Suicide Prevention Action Network USA
http://www.spanusa.org

Young Money
http://www.youngmoney.com
This Web site offers money management information that is aimed at young adults.

College and University Organizations

American Association of Community Colleges
http://www.aacc.nche.edu/

American Association of State Colleges and Universities
http://www.aascu.org/

American College Student Association
http://www.acsa.com/
Includes information on grants, scholarships, jobs, and student health insurance.

Association of American Colleges and Universities
http://www.aacu.org/

Association of American Universities
http://www.aau.edu/

BIBLIOGRAPHY

"A Guide to Scholarships." Education. *U.S. News & World Report.* August 19, 2004. Available online. URL: http://www.usnews.com/ usnews/edu/articles/040819/19sb_scholarships.htm. Accessed February 6, 2008.

Alcohol Policies Project: Center For Science in The Public Interest. "Fact Sheet: Binge Drinking on College Campuses." 2005. Available online. URL: http://www.cspinet.org/booze/collfact1.htm. Accessed January 20, 2008.

American College Health Association. *Sexually Transmitted Infections: What Everyone Should Know.* Baltimore: American College Health Association, 2006.

Association of Independent Colleges and Universities of Pennsylvania (AICUP). *Making the Case.* Harrisburg, Penn.: Association of Independent Colleges and Universities of Pennsylvania, 2006.

Atkinson, Richard. "College Admissions and the SAT: A Personal Perspective." *American Psychological Society* 18 (2005):15–22.

Barnett, Megan. "Mistakes Were Made." *U.S. News & World Report,* April 18, 2005. Available online. URL: http://www.usnews.com/ usnews/edu/articles/050418/18mistake.htm. Accessed January 20, 2008.

Barron's Educational Series. *Barron's Profiles of American Colleges.* Hauppauge, N.Y.: Barron's Educational Series, Inc. 27th ed. 2007.

Born, Jan, Bjorn Rasch, and Steffen Gals. "Sleep to Remember." *The Neuroscientist* 12 (2006): 410-424.

Brandon, Emily. "Don't Call It Negotiating." *U.S. News & World Report,* April 17, 2008. Available online.URL: http://www.usnews.com/ usnews/biztech/articles/060417/17negotiate.htm. Accessed January 7, 2008.

Bureau of Justice Statistics. *Drugs and Crime Facts.* Available online. URL: http://www.ojp.usdoj.gov/bjs/dcf/du.htm. Accessed Nov. 13, 2007.

Burns, David. *Feeling Good: The New Mood Therapy.* New York: Avon Books, 1992.

Butts, R. Freeman and Lawrence A. Cremin. *A History of Education in American Culture.* New York: Henry Holt and Company, 1953.

Callahan, Marion. "Prepping for College Life." *The Intelligencer.* August 15, 2005, 1A.

Campbell, David, Edward K. Strong, and Jo-Ida Hansen. *The Strong Interest Inventory.* Palo Alto, CA: Consulting Psychologists Press, 1991.

Centers for Disease Control and Prevention. "Cases of HIV Infection and AIDS in the United States and Dependent Areas, 2005 (Volume 17, revised edition)." Centers for Disease Control and Prevention. Available online. URL: http://www.cdc.gov/hiv/topics/surveillance/resources/reports/. Accessed January 20, 2008.

Clark, Kim. "College Tuition Prices Continue to Rise." *U.S. News & World Report,* October 23, 2007. Available online. URL: http://www.usnews.com/articles/business/paying-for-college/2007/10/23/college-tuition-prices-continue-to-rise.html. Accessed January 20, 2008.

Clark, Kim. "Report: Needy Students Got Less Scholarship Money." *U.S. News & World Report,* October 24, 2006. Available online. URL: http://www.usnews.com/usnews/biztech/articles/061024/24finaid.htm. Accessed January 20, 2008.

Clark, Kim. "Run the Numbers." *U.S. News & World Report,* April 8, 2007. Available online. URL: http://www.usnews.com/usnews/biztech/articles/070408/16intro.htm. Accessed January 20, 2008.

Clark, Kim. "Inside the Aid Office." *U.S. News & World Report,* April 8, 2007. Available online. URL: http://www.usnews.com/usnews/biztech/articles/070408/16pomona.htm?s_cid=related-links:TOP. Accessed January 20, 2008.

Clark, Kim. "An Admission Dean's Tips for Getting In." *U.S. News & World Report,* November 7, 2007. Available online. URL: http://www.usnews.com/articles/education/2007/11/07/an-admissions-deans-tips-for-getting-in.html. Accessed January 20, 2008.

Comeau, Ed (publisher). *Campus Firewatch: An Electronic Newsletter.* Available online. URL: http://www.campus-firewatch.com. Accessed January 20, 2008.

Conley, David T. *College Knowledge: What It Really Takes for Students to Succeed and What We Can Do to Get Them Ready.* San Francisco: Jossey-Bass, 2008.

Cross, Andrew. "Chlamydia Cases Hit Record High, Other STDs On the Rise." *The Daily Vidette,* Illinois State University, November 30, 2007. Available online. URL: http://media.www.dailyvidette .com/media/storage/paper420/news/2007/11/30/News/Chlamydia .Cases.In.U.S.Hit.Record.High.Other.Stds.On.The.Rise-3124637 .shtml. Accessed January 7, 2008.

Cushman, Kathleen. *First in the Family: Your College Years: Advice About College from First-Generation Students.* Providence, R.I.: Next Generation Press, 2005.

The Dormitory. "College Roommate Relations and Situations." *The Dormitory.* Available online. URL: http://www.thedormitoryonline .com/RoommateRelationsSituations.html. Accessed January 20, 2008.

Doster, William C. *CLEP 2008.* Hauppage, N.Y.: Barron's Educational Series, 2007.

Duckworth, Angela L. and Martin E.P. Seligman. "Self-Discipline Outdoes IQ in Predicting Academic Performance of Adolescents." *Psychological Science* 16 (2005): 939–944.

Ewers, Justin. "Is AP Too Good To Be True?" *U.S. News & World Report,* September 19, 2005. Available online. URL http:// www.usnews.com/usnews/edu/articles/050919/19advanced.htm. Accessed January 20, 2008.

Federal Student Aid Information Center. "Military Scholarships." *Student Aid on the Web.* Available online. URL: https://student aid.ed.gov/students/attachments/siteresources/74.pdf. Accessed January 20, 2008.

Feibish, Ashley. "Meningitis Becomes More Common on College Campuses; Death Rate High." *The Pendulum,* September 23, 2004. Available online. URL: http://www.elon .edu/e-web/pendulum/Issues/2004/9_23/news/meninigitis.xhtml. Accessed January 20, 2008.

Fifield, Adam. "Stay or Go?—Freshmen Can Be Quick to Switch Schools." *The Philadelphia Inquirer*, January 30, 2006, C1.

Fischman, Josh E. "Shots, Sex, and Safety." *U.S. News & World Report*, April 3, 2006. Available online. URL: http://health.usnews.com/usnews/health/articles/060326/3vaccine.b.htm. Accessed February 6, 2008.

Fischman, Josh E. "Sticking It to Cancer." *U.S. News & World Report*, March 26, 2006. Available online. URL: http://health.usnews.com/usnews/health/articles/060403/3vaccine.htm. Accessed February 6, 2008.

Fiske, Edward B. and Bruce G. Hammond. *What To Do When For College*, 4th ed. Naperville, Ill.: Source Books, 2007.

"Fraternities and Sororities" (by Roger B. Winston) *MSN Encarta*. Available online. URL: http://encarta.msn.com/encyclopedia_761575922/fraternitiesandsorenities.html. Accessed January 20, 2008.

Friedman, Thomas L. *The World is Flat: A Brief History of the Twenty-first Century*. New York: Farrar, Straus and Giroux, 2006.

Gallagher, Robert. *A National Survey of College Counseling Center Directors*. International Association of Counseling Services Inc., Monograph Series No. 8P (2006).

Gutek, Gerald. *Education in the United States: An Historical Perspective*. Englewood Cliffs, N.J.: Prentice Hall, 1986.

Heron, Helen H. *College Countdown: A Planning Guide for High School Students*. Livermore, Calif.: Heron Publishers, 2000.

Holland, John, Amy Powell, and Barbara Fritzche. *The Self-Directed Search*. Odessa, Fla.: Psychological Assessment Resources, 1994.

Johnston, Lloyd D., Patrick M. O'Malley, Jerald G. Bachman, and John E. Schulenberg. *Monitoring the Future National Survey Results on Drug Use, 1975–2005. Volume II: College Students and Adults Ages 19–45* (NIH Publication No. 06-5884). Bethesda, Md.: National Institute on Drug Abuse, pp. 227–276. Available online. URL: http://www.monitoringthefuture.org/pubs/monographs/vol2_2005.pdf. Accessed January 20, 2008.

Kadison, Richard and Theresa Foy Di Geronimo. *College of the Overwhelmed: The Campus Mental Health Crisis and What To Do About It.* San Francisco: Jossey-Bass, 2004.

Kirst, Michael and Andrea Veriezia. *From High School To College: Improving Opportunities for Success in Postsecondary Education.* San Francisco: Jossey-Bass, 2004.

Kronholz, June. "Colleges Get Building Fever." *Wall Street Journal,* May 18, 2005, B1. Available online. URL: http://www.realestate journal.com/propertyreport/newsandtrends/20050519-kronholz .html. Accessed January 20, 2008.

Leonard, Michael J. "Major Decisions: Some Common Misperceptions About Choosing A Major." *Penn State.* Available online. URL: http://www.psu.edu/dus/md/mdmisper.htm. Accessed January 20, 2008.

Lim, Paul J. "Savings 101: Changes to the Rules of 529 Plans Make Them More Attractive from a Financial Aid Standpoint." *U.S. News & World Report,* April 17, 2006: 70–71.

Lim, Paul J. "Nickel and Diming Your Kids to College," *U.S. News & World Report,* September 17, 2007, 57.

Litt, Ann Selkowitz. *The College Student's Guide to Eating Well on Campus.* Bethseda, Md.: Tulip Hill Press, 2000.

Loken, Eric, Filip Radinski, Vincent Crespi, and Josh Millet. "New SAT Is to Old SAT as...Researchers Look at Trends in Student Preparation for the New Version of the Test." *American Psychological Society* 18 (2005): 15–16.

Manahan, Samantha. "Estimating College Costs." *Intouch Newsletter,* New York Life Insurance Co. 57 (Summer 2005): 2.

Mansfield, Harvey C. "Grade Inflation: It's Time to Face the Facts." *The Chronicle of Higher Education,* April 6, 2001. Available online. URL: http://chronicle.com/weekly/v47/i30/30b02401.htm. Accessed January 20, 2008.

Marklein, Mary Beth. "Binge Drinking's Campus Toll." *USA Today,* September 7, 2005. Available online. URL: http://www.usatoday .com/news/health/child/2002-02-28campus-binge-drinking.htm. Accessed January 20, 2008.

Matlin, Margaret. *Cognition.* Fort Worth, Tex.: Harcourt Brace Jovanovich, 1994.

Mathews, Jay. "Test Wars." *Newsweek,* August 21, 2006. Available online. URL: http://www.newsweek.com/id/46418. Accessed February 6, 2008.

Merrow, John. "Declining by Degrees." *Carnegie Foundation For the Advancement of Teaching.* May 5, 2005, Available online. URL: http://www.carnegiefoundation.org/conversations/sub .asp?key=244&subkey=230. Accessed January 20, 2008.

Morse, Robert J. and Samuel Flanigan. "How the College Rankings Work." *U.S. News & World Report,* August 27, 2007, 110. Available online. URL: http://www.usnews.com/usnews/edu/articles/070819/27method.htm. Accessed January 20, 2008.

"MTV Network Increasing Mental Health Awareness at College Campuses." *Psychiatric Times.* 23, 14 (Dec. 1, 2006): 49. Available online. URL: http://www.psychiatrictimes.com/showArticle.jhtml?articleID=196602126. Accessed February 6, 2008.

Naab-Levy, Nikki. "The Yellow Line: Women Don't Know What They Risk When Binge Drinking." *The Post,* November 7, 2007. Available online. URL: http://www.thepost.ohiou.edu/Articles/Opinion/2007/11/07/22133/. Accessed January 20, 2008.

Niles, Spencer and JoAnn Harris-Bowlsbey. *Career Development Interventions in the 21st Century.* Upper Saddle River, N.J: Pearson, 2002.

Noble, Stuart. *History of American Education.* New York: Rinehart, 1954.

Orman, Suze. "For Student Loans, First Check with Uncle Sam." *The Philadelphia Inquirer,* September 2, 2007, M2. Available online. URL: http://www.philly.com/philly/phillywomen/9451577.html. Accessed January 20, 2008.

Palmer, Kimberly. "Loans Are as Tricky as Ever," *U.S. News & World Report,* September 17, 2007, 50. Available online. URL: http://www.usnews.com/articles/business/paying-for-college/2007/09/07/loans-are-as-tricky-as-ever.html. Accessed January 20, 2008.

Palmberg, Jennifer. "How to Pick a Major That is Right for You." *The Collegian,* August 29, 2005. Available online. URL: http://collegian

.csufresno.edu/archive/2005/08/29/features/major.shtml. Accessed February 6, 2008.

Peterson, Pamela. *Date Rape Drugs*. Scotts Valley, Calif.: ETR Associates brochure, 2004.

Prediger, Dale, "Aid for Mapping Occupations and Interests: A Graphic for Vocational Guidance and Research." *Vocational Guidance Quarterly* 30 (1981): 21–36.

Quinn, Jane Bryant. "New Math for College Costs," *Newsweek,* March 13, 2006, 43. Available online. URL: http://www.newsweek.com/id/46911. Accessed January 20, 2008.

Rodgers, Michael and David A. Starrett. "TECHPED: Don't Be Left in the E-Dust." *The Stanford University Center for Teaching and Learning.* November 14, 2005. Available online. URL: http://ctl.stanford.edu/Tomprof/postings/680.html. Accessed January 20, 2008.

Ruiz, Don Miguel. *The Four Agreements: A Practical Guide to Personal Freedom, A Toltec Wisdom Book.* San Rafael, Calif.: Amber-Allen Publishing, 1997.

Sander, Libby. "Student Aid Is Up, but College Costs have Risen Faster, Surveys Find." *Chronicle of Higher Education* 54 (2007): A26.

Schwartz, Barry. *The Paradox of Choice: Why More Is Less.* New York: HarperCollins, 2005.

Schwartz, Barry, Andrew Ward, John Monterosso, Sonja Lyobominski, Katherine White, and Darrin Lehman. "Maximizing Versus Satisficing: Happiness Is a Matter of Choice." *Journal of Personality and Social Psychology* 83 (2002): 1178–1197.

Schwartz, Stuart and Craig Conley. *Diverse Learners in the Classroom.* Boston: McGraw-Hill Primus, 2002.

Shellenbarger, Sue. "Colleges Ward Off Overinvolved Parents." *The Wall Street Journal,* July 28, 2005. Available online. URL: http://www.careerjournal.com/columnists/workfamily/20050729-work family.html. Accessed January 21, 2008.

SmartMoney.com. "Comparing Financial Aid Offers." Channel 3000–WISC TV. Available online. URL: http://www.channel3000.com/money/8037452/detail.html. Accessed January 20, 2008.

Thacker, Lloyd. *College Unranked: Ending the College Admissions Frenzy.* Cambridge, Mass.: Harvard University Press, 2005.

TIAA-CREF. "4 Advantages of 529 College Savings Plans." Fall 2005: 26.

Umbach, Paul and George Kuh. "Student Experiences with Diversity at Liberal Arts Colleges: Another Claim for Distinctiveness." *Journal of Higher Education* 77 (2006): 169–192.

U.S. Department of Education. *Preparing Your Child for College, A Resource Book for Parents.* 2000 Edition. Available online. URL: http://www.ed.gov/pubs/Prepare/index.html. Accessed January 20, 2008.

U.S. Department of Education. *The Student Guide: Financial Aid from the U.S. Department of Education.* Federal Student Aid Information Center, Washington D.C., 2007.

U.S. Department of Health and Human Services. "Psychoactive Stimulants." Available online. URL: http://www.nida.nih.gov/info fax/rohypnolGHB.html. Accessed February 6, 2008.

U.S. Department of Health and Human Services. "Substance Abuse Prevention." Available online. URL: http://www.ncadi.samhsa.gov/govpubs/prevalert/v3i28.aspx. Accessed January 21, 2008.

U.S. Department of Health and Human Services, National Institute on Drug Abuse. "NIDA Info Facts: Rohypnol and GHB," Washington, DC: U.S. Government Printing Office. September 24, 2002. Available online. URL: http://www.nida.nih.gov/Infofax/RohypnolGHB.html. Accessed January 21, 2007.

U.S. Department of Health and Human Services, National Institute on Drug Abuse. "NIDA Info Facts: MDMA (Ecstasy)," Washington, DC: U.S. Government Printing Office. September 24, 2002. Available online. URL: http://www.nida.nih.gov/Infofacts/ecstasy .html. Accessed January 21, 2008.

U.S. Department of Health and Human Services. SAMHSA's Center for Substance Abuse Prevention. Prevention Alert: Club Drugs: Ketamine Volume 3, Number 28 Washington, D.C.: U.S. Government Printing Office. Available online. URL: http://ncadi .samhsa.gov/govpubs/prevalent/v3i28.aspx. Accessed January 21, 2008.

U.S. Department of Justice. Office of Justice Programs. URL: http://
www.ed.gov/admins/lead/safety/handbook.pdf Accessed December
23, 2007.

U.S. Department of Labor, Bureau of Labor Statistics. *Occupational
Outlook Handbook*. 2006–2007 Edition. Available online. URL:
http://www.bls.gov/OCO/. Accessed January 20, 2008.

Weiss, Chlesea and Katie Uhlan. "How to Survive Parties." *The Daily
Campus*, February 7, 2005. Available online. URL: http://media.www
.dailycampus.com/media/storage/paper340/news/2005/02/07/
Focus/How-To.Survive.Parties-854842-page2.shtml. Accessed
February 6, 2008.

Welsh, Mary Jeanne, Chairperson, Department of Accounting, La
Salle University, Philadelphia, Penn., in a discussion with the
authors, May 25, 2007.

A

accidents. *See* automobile accidents
acquaintance rape, 145
ACT. *See* American College Test
active learning, 104, 110–111
active reading, 95–96
addiction, 152, 158
admissions process, 81–97
advanced placement (AP) courses, 19, 28, 84, 99–100
aid. *See* financial aid
alcohol, 128–129, 139–140, 153–156, 160
Ali, Muhammad, 121
Alito, Rose, 99
American College Health Association, 140
American College Test (ACT), 88, 89, 91
Americorps, 35
amphetamines, 158–159
analytical thinking, 107–108
anorexia nervosa, 151
AP courses. *See* advanced placement courses
appeals, in financial aid process, 46
application process, 82–88

applied knowledge, 94–97
athletics, 77, 131–132
athletic scholarships, 33–34
automobile accidents, 74–75, 139–140, 142–143

B

background check, 82–83
barbiturates, 157–158
binge drinking, 129, 130, 153–155
binge eating disorder, 151–152
body image, 149–151
Brown, Claude, 167
bulimia, 151
Burns, David D., 136

C

caffeine, 153
campus visit, 16, 76–79
career counselors, 59–61
career planning, 51–62, 72
Carlyle, Thomas, 51
Carnegie, Dale, 81
Case, Joe Paul, 46
cell phones, 136
change
of college, 79–80
of major, 55–56
Churchill, Winston, 168–169

cigarettes, 152
Civil Rights Act (1964), 165
clarity, in writing, 106–107
class attendance, 100
class participation, 103
class size, 63, 64, 66, 112
CLEP (College-Level Examination Program), 28
Clery Act, 75, 141
club drugs, 159–160
cocaine, 158
college(s), universities vs., 64–65, 112
College Board, 88–89
college career counselors, 61
College-Level Examination Program (CLEP), 28
college preparatory schools, 99
College Savings Plans Network (CSPN), 42
Columbia University, 11
The Common Application, 83
community colleges, 27, 73–74
community service. *See* service learning
community service scholarships, 34
commuting student, 69–70

competitive colleges, 13–14, 65–66
Comprehensive Articulation Agreement, 27
compromise, 127
concentration, 90
co-operative study program, 71–72
Cornell University, 76
cost, of college, 12, 18, 23–49
cost of attendance, 38, 47
counselors, 59–61, 148–149
Coverdell ESAs. *See* Educational and Savings Accounts
crack cocaine, 158
credit (financial), 135
credit cards, 135
crime, 74–75, 82–83, 141–142
critical reading, 94
CSPN (College Savings Plans Network), 42
cultural activities, 70–71
curriculum, 67–69

D

date rape, 145, 160
direct loans, 47
Direct PLUS Loans, 38
Direct Stafford Loan, 37
disabilities, students with, 144
discipline. *See* self-discipline
disease. *See* infectious disease

distance learning, 74
diversity, 49, 124
dormitory life, 127–128
drinking. *See* alcohol
drug/alcohol use, 139–140, 145, 151–161
dual major, 56
Duckworth, Angela, 17

E

eating disorders, 150–151
economic diversity, 49
economic opportunity, 118
Edison, Thomas, 99
Educational and Savings Accounts (ESAs), 41
EFC. *See* Expected Family Contribution
Einstein, Albert, 63, 163
Emerson, Ralph Waldo, 139
emotional abuse, 147
emotional maturity, 117–119
emotional problems. *See* mental health
employee scholarships/discounts, 34
"environmental press," 65
ESAs (Educational and Savings Accounts), 41
essay tests, 94, 95
exams, 102–103
excuses, 114
exercise, 142, 144
Expected Family Contribution, (EFC) 30, 43, 47

extracurricular activities, 19, 130

F

Facebook, 128
FAFSA. *See* Free Application for Federal Student Aid
failure, fear of, 104
family, 1, 57–59
Federal Direct Student Loan Program (FDSLP), 47
Federal Family Education Loan Program (FFELP), 37, 38, 47
Federal Income Tax Reduction Act (1997), 35–36
Federal Supplemental Educational Opportunity Grants (FSEOG), 31
FFELP. *See* Federal Family Education Loan Program
financial aid, 19, 20, 29–35, 43–47
fire safety, 141
529 College Savings Plans, 41–42
foreign countries, study in, 72–73
The Four Agreements (Ruiz), 118
fraternities, 130–131, 141
Free Application for Federal Student Aid (FAFSA), 30, 43, 47
Friedman, Thomas, 107–108, 163
friends, 14, 125–126

FSEOG (Federal
  Supplemental
  Educational
  Opportunity Grants),
  31
fulfillment, work and,
  62, 119

G

gambling, 129
gender discrimination,
  164–165
GHB, 159, 160
G.I. Bill, 164
glass ceiling, 165
grade point average
  (GPA), 136–137
grades, 103–104, 113,
  130–131
graduation, in four vs.
  five years, 24–27
grants, 30–31, 44–45
Great Depression,
  164

H

hallucinogens, 159
hashish, 157
hazing, 130
health and safety,
  139–161
health insurance, 140
Heckman, James,
  48–49
"helicopter parents,"
  135
high school, 11,
  18–20, 100
high-school
  counselors, 59–60
high school record, 82
HIV/AIDS, 145
home equity loans,
  38–39

hookah, 152
Hope Tax Credit, 35

I

illness. *See* infectious
  disease
income, of college
  graduates, 23, 25
infectious disease,
  140–141
initial learning,
  108–109
inspiration, sources of,
  165–166
in-state tuition,
  27–28
Integrated
  Postsecondary
  Education Data
  System (IPEDS), 26
intellectual
  development, 122
Internal Revenue
  Service, 35
international
  programs, 72–73
Internet, 74, 116–117,
  128
internships, 71–72
interviews, 87–88
investment, college
  education as, 23, 64
IPEDS (Integrated
  Postsecondary
  Education Data
  System), 26

J

junior colleges, 27

K

ketamine, 159–160
knowledge, as power,
  118

Kronholz, June, 77
Kuh, George, 49

L

LaSalle University, 25,
  55–56
learning
  active, 110–111
  resources for,
    113–115
  self-discipline and,
    104, 105
  sleep deprivation
    and, 143
  study skills and,
    108–110
learning-to-learn
  concept, 105–106
letters of
  recommendation,
  85–86
liberal arts education,
  56–57
librarians, 115
life skills, 134
Lifetime Learning Tax
  Credit, 35
Lincoln, Abraham, 133
Lindbergh, Anne
  Morrow, 163
loans, 36–39, 45, 132
location of college,
  15, 70
Louisiana State
  University, 146
love. *See* relationships

M

Maguire, Maired, 163
major, selection of,
  53–59, 72, 119
*Manchild in the
  Promised Land*
  (Brown), 167

marijuana, 156–157
Marx, Groucho, 81
mathematics,
  standardized tests for,
  91–93
maturity, emotional,
  117–119
MDMA, 159
medication, and test
  preparation, 89
memorization, 109,
  110
men
  and body image, 149
  drug/alcohol use,
  129
  in first year of
  college, 102
mental health,
  147–149
mentors, 125
merit-based
  scholarships, 33
methamphetamines,
  158–159
methodology, 107
minorities, 124
minors, 56
mission statement, 66
mistakes, in college
  selection/preparation,
  11–21
money. See cost, of
  college
money management,
  134–135
moral development,
  133–134
Mullendore, Richard,
  136
multiple-choice tests,
  90
mutual funds, 42
MySpace, 128

N
Nash, Ogden, 63
National Merit
  Scholarships, 31–33
need-based financial
  aid, 29–30
New York Times, 15
nicotine, 152
note taking, 111

O
obesity, 150–151
The Occupational
  Outlook Handbook
  (U.S. Department of
  Labor), 51
October Sky (film), 167
opiates, 158
overeating, 143–144

P
papers, writing, 115–
  117
The Paradox of Choice
  (Schwartz), 1
parents, 3, 17–18,
  135–136
parties, 128–129
part-time job, 132
Pasqua, Elaine, 153–
  154
paying for college. See
  cost, of college
Pell Grants, 30–31, 48
The Pendulum (Elon
  College newspaper),
  140
perfectionism, 14–15,
  136–137
Perkins loans, 36–37,
  48
perseverance, 168–169
personal development,
  121–125

personal statement,
  84–85
plagiarism, avoiding,
  117
PLUS loans, 38, 39,
  45, 48
potential,
  underemphasizing
  your, 16–17
pregnancy, 146
prejudices, 133–134
Preliminary SAT/
  National Merit
  Scholarship
  Qualifying Test
  (PSAT/NMSQT), 20,
  31–32, 88, 91
prep school, 99
prestige,
  overemphasizing,
  12–14
priorities, 167–168
private colleges, cost
  of, 23–24
private professional
  career counselors,
  60–61
problems, analyzing,
  107–108
procrastination, 15,
  16, 115–116
professional journals,
  116, 117
professors, 66–67,
  111–113
PSAT/NMSQT.
  See Preliminary
  SAT/National
  Merit Scholarship
  Qualifying Test
psychological
  problems, 147–149
public colleges, 23–24
punctuality, 87, 113

Q

questions
  to clarify reading,
    111
  importance of,
    107–108
  to test your own
    knowledge of
    subject, 110
quotations, in papers,
  117

R

RA (residence
  advisor), 128
Rabi, Isidor I.,
  107–108
rape, 145, 153
reading, 95–96, 106
recommendations.
  See letters of
  recommendation
Redd, Kenneth, 46
reference librarians,
  115
relationships,
  146–147
relearning, 96–97, 109
religious affiliation, of
  college, 68
Reserve Officer
  Training Corps
  scholarships. *See*
  ROTC scholarships
residence advisor,
  (RA) 128
resident student,
  69–70
respect, friendship
  and, 126
responsibilities,
  100–103
reviewing, as study
  skill, 109

risk, 122
Rogers, Michael L., 2
Rogers, Will, 163
Rohypnol (roofies),
  160
role models, 125
romantic relationships.
  See relationships
roommates, 126–127
Roosevelt, Eleanor,
  121
ROTC (Reserve
  Officer Training
  Corps) scholarships,
  35
Ruiz, Don Miguel,
  118
rural campus, 70

S

safety, 139–161
SAR (Student Aid
  Report), 43, 48
SAT. *See* Scholastic
  Aptitude Test
saving, for college,
  39–42
scholarships, 31–35,
  44–45
Scholastic Aptitude
  Test (SAT), 88–89,
  91–93
Schwartz, Barry, 1
Schweitzer, Albert, 51
second-choice college,
  79–80
selection interview,
  87–88
self-acceptance,
  123–124
self-determination,
  121
Self-Directed Search,
  52

self-discipline,
  100–102, 104, 105
self-esteem, 118–119
self-improvement,
  124–125
self-knowledge,
  122–123
Seligman, Martin, 17
senior year, of high
  school, 19–20
SEOG (Supplemental
  Educational
  Opportunity Grants),
  48
service learning,
  132–133
Seton Hall University,
  141
sex, unprotected, 154
sexuality, 144–146
sexually transmitted
  diseases, (STDs)
  145–146, 154
Shellenbarger, Sue,
  124
sleep, and test
  preparation, 89
sleep deprivation,
  142–143
smoke alarms, 141
smoking, 152
social development
  at college, 69–70,
  121–138
social life, 67–71
sororities, 130–131,
  141
sources, evaluating,
  116–117
Stafford loans, 36–39,
  45, 48
standardized tests,
  16–17, 81, 88–97
Starrett, David A., 2

state schools. *See*
  public colleges
STDs (sexually
  transmitted diseases),
  145–146, 154
stress, 13–14, 16, 18,
  148, 155
Strong Interest
  Inventory, 52
Student Aid Report
  (SAR), 43, 48
student-teacher ratio.
  See class size
study-abroad
  opportunities, 72–73
study skills, 108–111
style *vs.* substance,
  14, 63–64, 77–78
Subsidized FFEL, 37
subsidized loans, 48
substance-free
  housing, 156
success, perfection *vs.*,
  136
suicide, 147–148
summer courses, 29
summer job, 132
Supplemental
  Educational
  Opportunity Grants
  (SEOG), 48
Swift, Jonathan, 11

T
taxes/tax credits,
  35–36, 41–42
teaching assistants
  (TAs), 63, 64, 103
teaching quality, 16,
  66–67, 77–78
teaching styles,
  110–111

tests, 102–103. *See
  also* standardized
  tests
theft, 75
time, in classroom,
  100–101
time management, 91
tobacco, 152
tranquilizers, 157–158
transcript, 82, 84
transferring, 79
Travel Study Courses,
  73
tuition. *See* cost, of
  college
two-for-one deals, 29
two-year programs,
  27

U
Umbach, Paul, 49
understanding,
  memorizing *vs.*, 110
U.S. Armed Forces, 35
university(ies),
  colleges *vs.*, 64–65,
  112
University of Vermont,
  136
university-specific
  scholarships, 33, 34
unmet need, 48
unprotected sex,
  alcohol and, 154
unsubsidized loan, 48
urban campus, 70, 74
*U.S. News & World
  Report,* 30, 36, 75

V
vaccinations, 140
veterans' benefits, 35

visit, to prospective
  college, 16, 76–79
vocabulary building,
  94–95
volunteer work,
  84–85. *See also*
  service learning

W
Welsh, Mary Jeanne,
  25
Wilde, Oscar, 23
wisdom, knowledge
  vs., 118
women
  anorexia nervosa,
    150
  body image, 149
  drug use, 129
  educational
    advances, 164–165
  first year of college,
    102
  and "freshman 15,"
    143
  problem drinking,
    129, 154
work, to defray college
  costs, 39, 45–46, 48,
  132
work habits, 16–17,
  100, 104–105
Work-Study Program,
  39
The World Is Flat
  (Friedman),
  107–108
World War, II 164
writing, 93–94,
  106–107, 115–117

ABOUT THE AUTHORS

John J. Rooney, Ph.D. is emeritus professor in the Department of Psychology and director of the master's program in clinical counseling psychology at LaSalle University in Philadelphia, Pennsylvania. He has also served as chair, director of the Counseling Center, and president of the Faculty Senate at LaSalle University. Dr. Rooney instituted one of the earliest, pre-college counseling programs designed to assist students in their transition from high school to college and developed an Inventory of Habits of Study and Attitudes Toward College, which has demonstrated value in predicting student retention and achievement. He has served as president of both the Personnel and Guidance Association of Greater Philaderlphia and the Academic Division of the Pennsylvania Psychological Association. Dr. Rooney has published research, conducted workshops, and presented scholarly papers. He has also published in popular and literary outlets. In addition, he has been a guest on radio and television, is a frequent book reviewer for *The Philadelphia Inquirer*, and is regularly interviewed for nationally circulated news articles. In 2008 he was selected to receive the John P. Dondero Memorial Award for "making the science and practice of psychology accessible to others in their search for humanistically and spiritually directed lives."

John F. Reardon, Ed.D. is emeritus professor in the Department of Accounting at LaSalle University and chaired the department from 1991 to 2000. Dr. Reardon visits high schools to speak to students about preparing for college. For the school year 2006-2007 he spoke at more than 40 high schools. He has spoken at nearly 60 in the 2007-2008 school year. Dr. Reardon was one of seven faculty selected nationally by Arthur Andersen & Company to participate in their first faculty internship program in Chicago in 1965. He received the

Lindback Award for Distinguished Teaching in 1969, the Tau Kappa Epsilon's Man of the Year Award in 1984, the Doctor Roland Holyroyd Award in 1986, and LaSalle University's Yearbook Dedication in 1987. Dr. Reardon was Trueblood Scholar with Deloitte/Touche public accounting firm in 1991 and out of 31 participants, was one of 12 selected to present at the conference in Scottsdale, Arizona. Dr. Reardon was the recipient of the inaugural Provost's Award for Distinguished Faculty in 1999 and the John J. Finley Memorial Award in 2002. The Jack Reardon Learning Center was dedicated to Dr. Reardon in 2003.